NEW YORK ARCHITECTURE

NEW YORK ARCHITECTURE

F K G

F K G

Editorial project:
2010 © LOFT Publications
Via Laietana, 32, 4.º, Of. 92
08003 Barcelona, Spain
Tel.: +34 932 688 088
Fax: +34 932 687 073
loft@loftpublications.com
www.loftpublications.com

Created and distributed in cooperation with Frechmann Kolón GmbH
www.frechmann.com

Editor:
Daniela Santos Quartino

Editorial coordinator:
Simone K. Schleifer

Assistant to editorial coordination:
Aitana Lleonart

Art director:
Mireia Casanovas Soley

Design and layout coordination:
Claudia Martínez Alonso

Cover layout:
Nacho Gràcia Blanco

Layout:
Yolanda G. Román

Translations:
Equipo de Edición

ISBN:
978-84-92731-07-7 (INT)
978-80-556-0011-6 (SLOVART)

Printed in China

Cover photo:
Patrick Petruchelli

The American Dream is what drives New York, a city which is not stopped by threats and which knows no limits. Manhattan Island develops vertically and, in its eagerness to touch the sky, contemporary architecture comes in shapes and structures which could be straight out of the realms of science fiction.

From the skyscrapers and the lofts which occupy the brick buildings in Downtown New York, to the new elevated gardens on the urban map and the planned ecological constructions which form part of the scheme to convert New York into a green city by 2030, this book presents the transformations which are taking place in the metropolis. It also features the neo-Gothic, Art Deco and Rationalism buildings which have contributed to molding the booming, revolutionary character that represents one of the most vibrant cities on the planet.

Der amerikanische Traum ist der Antriebsmotor von New York, einer Stadt, die keine Grenzen kennt und sich von nichts und niemandem einschüchtern lässt. Vor allem Manhattan wächst unablässig in die Höhe, und in diesem Streben nach dem Himmel bringt die zeitgenössische Architektur Formen und Strukturen hervor, die direkt aus der Zukunft zu kommen scheinen.

In diesem Buch finden sich die großen Wolkenkratzer ebenso wie die Lofts in den Backsteinhäusern der Downtown, die überall entstehenden Dachgärten und die ökologischen Gebäude, die New York im Jahre 2030 zu einer grünen Stadt machen sollen. Gezeigt werden die ständigen Veränderungen der Metropole, aber auch jene neugotischen Bauten oder die Meisterwerke des Art Déco und des Rationalismus, die kennzeichnend sind für den revolutionären Schwung und den unbändigen Vorwärtsdrang einer der lebendigsten Städte der Welt.

Le rêve américain est le moteur de New York, une ville qui ne recule pas devant les menaces et ne connaît aucune limite. L'île de Manhattan se développe en hauteur et, dans l'envie de toucher le ciel, l'architecture contemporaine apparaît avec des formes et des structures qui semblent sortir tout droit d'un film de science-fiction.

Des gratte-ciel et des lofts situés dans les immeubles en brique du Downtown aux nouveaux jardins en hauteur de la carte urbaine, en passant par les futurs bâtiments écologiques du projet qui prévoit de transformer New York en une ville verte en 2030, ce livre présente les transformations en cours dans la métropole. Le tout, sans oublier les bâtiments néo-gothiques, Art déco ou rationalistes, qui ont contribué à façonner le caractère vigoureux et révolutionnaire qui caractérise une des villes les plus vibrantes de la planète.

The American Dream is de motor van New York, een stad die zich niet stil laat leggen door bedreigingen en die geen grenzen kent. Manhattan groeit in opwaartse richting. In deze drang om de hemel aan te raken komt de hedendaagse architectuur met vormen en structuren die pure sciencefiction lijken.

Dit boek laat de veranderingen zien die zich in de metropool voordoen: van de wolkenkrabbers en de *lofts* in de bakstenen gebouwen in Downtown New York tot de nieuwe verhoogde parken dwars door de stad heen, evenals de toekomstige milieuvriendelijke gebouwen die deel uitmaken van een plan om New York in 2030 een groene stad te laten zijn. In dit boek zijn ook neogotische gebouwen en gebouwen in rationalistische en art-decostijl te zien; ze hebben bijgedragen aan het bloeiende, revolutionaire karakter van New York, een van de levendigste steden ter wereld.

(1) DOWNTOWN

(2) MIDTOWN

(3) UPTOWN

(4) BOROUGHS

DOWNTOWN

LIVE

Blue Residential Tower 1

105 Norfolk Street

Bernard Tschumi Architects
www.tschumi.com

© Peter Mauss/Esto

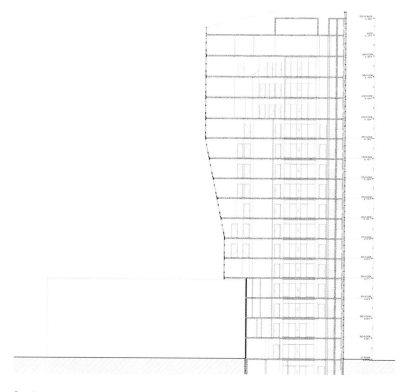

Section

Varying shades of blue make up the façade of this 16-storey building, which was constructed like a curious pixel image of angled surfaces – a sculptural shape which the architects created to comply with the complex building laws in the area.

Abstufungen verschiedener Blautöne beherrschen die Fassade dieses 16stöckigen Hochhauses. Die auffällig kantige Bauform des Gebäudes, das wie eine Skulptur wirkt, ergab sich aus den komplexen baupolizeilichen Vorschriften in dieser Gegend.

Différents tons de bleu composent la façade de cette tour de 16 étages, construite comme une curieuse image pixélisée avec des surfaces angulaires. C'est une forme sculpturale, créée par les architectes en fonction de la législation complexe de la construction dans ce secteur.

De verschillende tinten blauw bepalen de gevel van deze toren van zestien verdiepingen. Het gebouw rijst op als een soort sculptuur, een opvallend object van hoekige pixelvlakken. De architecten kwamen tot dit resultaat om tegemoet te komen aan de complexe bouwverordeningen die in de omgeving golden.

LIVE

Five Franklin Place ②

5 Franklin Place

UNStudio
www.unstudio.com

Drawings: © UNStudio

This 20-storey residential building will be located over Franklin Place, a narrow paved street, dating back to the 19th century, in the Tribeca area. The building is wrapped in a skin made up of black metallic bands that appear to be woven together and which form balconies and terraces.

Dieses Wohnhochhaus soll am Franklin Place entstehen, einer Straße des 19. Jhs. im Viertel Tribeca. Die Außenhaut des Gebäudes wird von schwarzen, scheinbar ineinander verflochtenen Metallbändern gebildet, die sich zu Balkons und Terrassen erweitern.

Cette tour résidentielle de 20 étages sera située sur Franklin Place, une ruelle pavée du XIXᵉ siècle, dans le quartier de Tribeca. Le bâtiment est enveloppé d'une « peau » de bandes métalliques noires qui donnent l'impression d'être tissées ensemble et forment balcons et terrasses.

Deze woontoren van twintig verdiepingen zal op Franklin Place komen te staan, een smalle straat in TriBeCa uit de 19e eeuw. Het gebouw krijgt een huid van zwarte stroken metaal die met elkaar verweven lijken en die de balkons en terrassen vormen.

LIVE

One Jackson Square ③

122 Greenwich Avenue

Kohn Pedersen Fox Associates
www.kpf.com

© John Chu

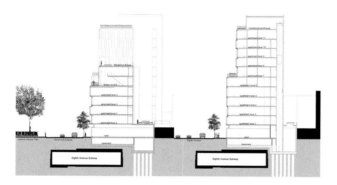

Sections

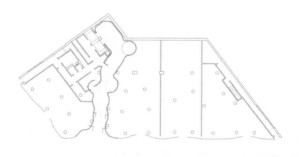

Ground floor plan

Second floor plan

Typical duplex floor plan

In this Greenwich Village building there are 35 luxury residences. Like strips of curved glass, each of the floors generates shapes which flow along the length of the façade. The gardens on the roofs connect the private environment of the homes with the public park.

Dieses Gebäude in Greenwich Village umfasst 35 Luxus-Wohnungen. Jedes Geschoss erscheint wie ein schwingendes gläsernes Band, das die Fassade entlang fließt. Über die auf den Dächern angelegten Gärten wird der Privatbereich mit einem öffentlichen Park verbunden.

Cet édifice situé à Greenwich Village comprend 35 résidences de luxe. Chaque étage, semblable à des bandes en verre formant des ondulations, génère des formes qui s'écoulent le long de la façade. Les jardins privés des demeures situés sur les toits établissent un lien visuel avec le jardin public.

In dit gebouw in Greenwich Village bevinden zich 35 luxewoningen. Als golvende stroken glas creëren de verdiepingen vormen over de hele breedte van de gevel. De tuinen op de daken verbinden de privéomgeving van de woningen met het openbare park.

SEE

New Museum of Contemporary Art ④

235 Bowery

Kazuyo Sejima + Ryue Nishizama/SANAA
www.sanaa.co.jp

© Wade Zimmerman

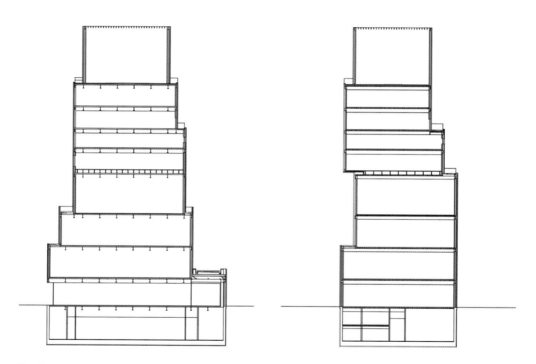

Elevations

Located in a densely urban area, this 174-foot-high building stands out with its white presence and shaped structure, which is made up of six rectangular blocks piled on top of each other, slightly off-center. The different heights allow light to flow into the building.

Dieses 53 Meter hohe Gebäude befindet sich in einem der am dichtesten besiedelten Teile der Stadt. Es sticht durch die weiße Farbe und seine Struktur hervor, die aus sechs unregelmäßig übereinander gestapelten rechteckigen Blöcken besteht. Durch die unterschiedlichen Höhen gelangt Tageslicht in die Räume.

Situé dans une zone à haute densité urbaine, ce bâtiment de 53 mètres de hauteur se distingue par sa présence blanche et sa structure formelle composée de six blocs rectangulaires empilés et légèrement décentrés. En raison des différences de hauteur, la lumière du jour peut y pénétrer.

Dit gebouw van 53 meter hoog staat in dicht stedelijk gebied en valt op door zijn witte kleur en zijn formele structuur, bestaande uit zes rechthoekige, gestapelde en licht afwijkend geplaatste blokken. Door de hoogteverschillen kan het daglicht naar binnen vallen.

LEARN

Cooper Union ⑤

41 Cooper Square

Morphosis Architects
www.morphosis.com

© Wade Zimmerman

ION

THE COOPER UNION

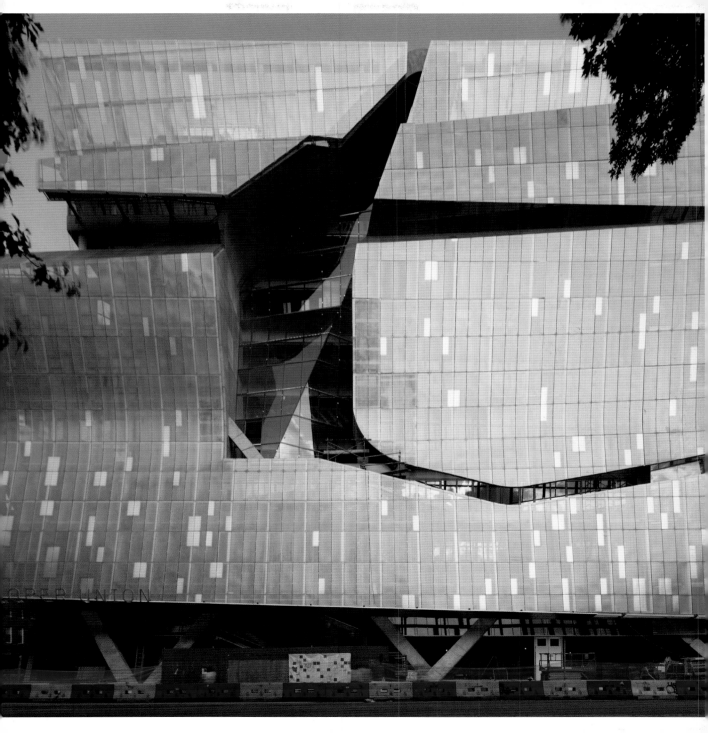

The new academic building for the Cooper Union – which teaches art, architecture, engineering, humanities and social sciences – has been designed like a vertical piazza contained within a semi-transparent wrapping. The sculptural façade connects the exterior with the heart of the building.

Das neue Lehrgebäude der Cooper Union für den Unterricht in Kunst, Architektur, Ingenieur-, Geistes- und Sozialwissenschaften wurde als eine Art senkrechter *Piazza* in einer halbdurchsichtigen Hülle entworfen. Die auffällig gestaltete Fassade verbindet die Außenwelt mit dem Herzen des Gebäudes.

Le nouveau bâtiment académique de The Cooper Union, consacré à l'enseignement de l'art, de l'architecture et de l'ingénierie, des sciences humaines et sociales, a été conçu comme une piazza verticale contenue dans une enveloppe semi-transparente. Sa façade sculpturale relie l'extérieur avec le cœur du bâtiment.

Het nieuwe academiegebouw van The Cooper Union, waar kunst, architectuur, technische, sociale en geesteswetenschappen worden onderwezen, is een soort verticale *piazza* die in een halfdoorzichtige verpakking gevat is. De sculpturale gevel verbindt het exterieur met het hart van het gebouw.

WORK

Goldman Sachs World Headquarters (6)

West Street at Vesey Street, Battery Park City

Henry Cobb / Pei Cobb Freed & Partners
www.pcf-p.com

© Wade Zimmerman

This 43-storey steel and glass building has been designed with the very latest in green technology, including the use of fuels with very low levels of sulfates. Outside, a commercial gallery will surround the first floor and will link once again the roads in the area with Hudson River Park.

Der Wolkenkratzer aus Glas und Stahl ist mit den neuesten Errungenschaften auf dem Gebiet der „grünen" Gebäudetechnik ausgestattet. Unter anderem wird nur Brennstoff mit extrem niedrigen Schwefelwerten verwendet. Die Ladengalerie im Erdgeschoss erschließt den Zugang zum Hudson River Park.

Cette tour de 43 étages en acier et en verre a été conçue avec la technologie la plus récente en termes de « bâtiments verts », y compris l'utilisation de carburant faible en sulfate. À l'extérieur, une galerie commerciale entourera le rez-de-chaussée et permettra de relier l'environnement avec le Hudson River Park.

Deze 43 verdiepingen hoge toren van staal en glas bezit de nieuwste 'groene' technologie, waaronder het gebruik van energie met uiterst lage sulfaatgehalten. Aan de buitenkant zal op de begane grond rondom een galerie komen en de omliggende wegen zullen in verbinding staan met het Hudson River Park.

WORK

World Trade Center ⑦

Church Street, Liberty Street, Barclay Street, Greenwich Street

Skidmore, Owings & Merrill; Santiago Calatrava; Norman Foster; Richard Rogers;
Maki and Associates; Michael Arad; Peter Walker; Davis Brody Bond; Snøhetta
www.wtc.com

Renderings: © courtesy of Silverstein Properties

Model shot

The new World Trade Center, to be built in the area where the Twin Towers stood, will be made up of six buildings which will provide almost 1 million square meters of space for offices (Freedom Tower or Tower 1, Towers 2, 3, 4 and 5, and the 7 WTC) as well as the National September 11 Memorial & Museum, WTC Transportation Hub, a commercial area and the Performing Arts Center.

Das neue World Trade Center auf dem Gelände, das früher die Zwillingstürme einnahmen, wird aus sechs Gebäuden bestehen, die fast eine Million Quadratmeter Bürofläche bieten (Freedom Tower bzw. Turm 1, die Türme 2, 3, 4 y 5, und das 7 WTC). Dazu kommen das National September 11 Memorial & Museum, der U-Bahnhof WTC Transportation Hub, ein Einkaufszentrum und das Performing Arts Center.

Le nouveau World Trade Center, dans l'espace occupé auparavant par les tours jumelles, se composera de six édifices qui fourniront presque un million de mètres carrés pour des bureaux (Freedom Tower ou Tour 1, les Tours 2, 3, 4 et 5 et le 7WTC), ainsi que le National September 11 Memorial & Museum, la station de métro WTC Transportation Hub, une zone commerciale et le Performing Arts Center.

Het nieuwe World Trade Center bestaat uit zes gebouwen die bijna een miljoen vierkante meter aan kantoren beslaan (Freedom Tower of Tower 1, Towers 2, 3, 4 en 5, en 7 WTC). Het huisvest het National September 11 Memorial & Museum, het metrostation WTC Transportation Hub, een winkelcentrum en het Performing Arts Center.

WORK

Tower 4 (8)

150 Greenwich Street

Maki and Associates
www.maki-and-associates.co.jp

Renderings: © Maki and Associates, courtesy of Silverstein Properties

This cement and steel building with a glass skin will be located in front of the WTC Memorial Park. Of its 64 storeys, 5 will be used for stores and the rest as offices. It will be the fourth highest building.

Dieser Turm aus Beton, Stahl und Glas soll gegenüber dem WTC Memorial Park entstehen. Von seinen 64 Stockwerken werden fünf für Läden und Geschäfte genutzt werden, die übrigen für Büroräume. Es handelt sich um den vierthöchsten Turm des Komplexes.

Cette tour en ciment et acier, avec un revêtement en verre, sera située en face du WTC Memorial Park. Elle comportera 64 étages, dont 5 seront destinés au commerce et le reste à des bureaux. Ce sera la quatrième tour la plus haute du quartier.

Deze toren van cement en staal met een huid van glas staat tegenover het WTC Memorial Park. Hij heeft 64 verdiepingen, waarvan vijf bestemd zijn voor winkels en de overige voor kantoren. Het is de op drie na hoogste toren van het gebied.

WORK

Tower 3 ⑨

175 Greenwich St

Richard Rogers/Rogers Stirk Harbour + Partners
www.richardrogers.co.uk

Renderings: © Rogers Stirk Harbour + Partners, courtesy of Silverstein Properties

This will be the third highest building in the World Trade Center, comprising 71 storeys – 54 of which will be used for offices and the rest for stores. It will be located in the center of the complex, close to the National September 11 Memorial & Museum.

Der dritthöchste Turm des World Trade Center wird 71 Stockwerke haben, von denen 54 Büros und die restlichen Geschäfte aufnehmen werden. Er entsteht im Zentrum des Gebäudekomplexes, in der Nähe des National September 11 Memorial & Museum.

Ce sera la troisième tour la plus haute du World Trade Center. Elle aura 71 étages, dont 54 destinés à des bureaux et le reste au commerce. Elle sera située au centre du complexe de bâtiments, très près du National September 11 Memorial & Museum.

Dit is de op twee na hoogste toren van het World Trade Center. Het gebouw telt 71 verdiepingen, waarvan 54 bestemd zijn voor kantoren. Op de overige verdiepingen komen winkels. Hij staat in het midden van het gebouwencomplex, dicht bij het National September 11 Memorial & Museum.

WORK

Tower 2 (10)

200 Greenwich Street

Foster and Partners
www.fosterandpartners.com

Renderings: © Foster and Partners, courtesy of Silverstein Properties

Sketch

This building, with its crystalline façade and diamond-shaped pinnacle, will have 78 floors and will be the second tallest building in the World Trade Center. It will be located east of the Performing Arts Center and north of the WTC Transportation Hub, with a 82-foot-high antenna on top.

Dieser Turm mit seiner gläsernen Fassade und der Spitze in Diamantenform zählt 78 Stockwerke und ist das zweithöchste Gebäude des World Trade Center. Er wird östlich neben dem Performing Arts Center, nördlich des WTC Transportation Hub entstehen und eine 25 Meter hohe Antenne tragen.

Cette tour, avec sa façade cristalline et son pinacle en forme de diamant, aura 79 étages et sera le deuxième édifice le plus haut du World Trade Center. Elle se situera à l'est du Performing Arts Center et au nord du WTC Transportation Hub. Au sommet sera installée une antenne de 25 mètres.

Deze toren met doorzichtige gevel en een diamantvormige pinakel heeft 78 verdiepingen en is het op één na hoogste gebouw van het World Trade Center. Hij ligt ten oosten van het Performing Arts Center en ten noorden van het WTC Transportation Hub. Op het hoogste punt staat een antenne van 25 meter.

WORK

7 World Trade Center (11)

250 Greenwich Street

SOM Skidmore, Owings & Merrill
www.som.com

© Ruggero Vanni; David Sundberg/Esto Photographics

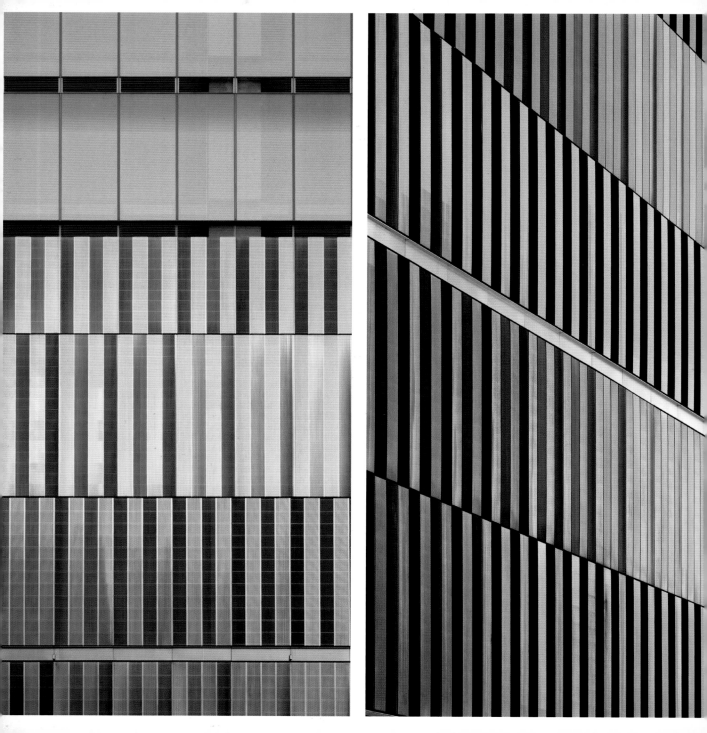

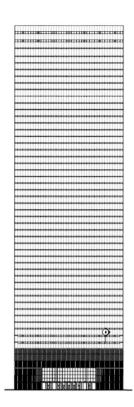

East elevation

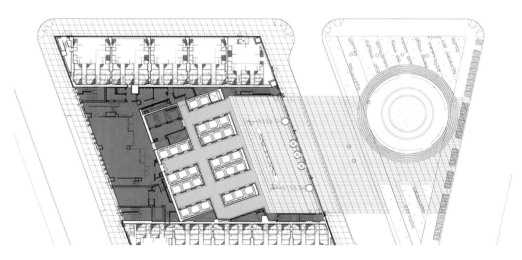

Ground floor plan

The first building to be constructed in the area adjacent to Ground Zero is a 52-storey skyscraper which marks the entrance to the World Trade Center complex. The surface of the new building was designed like a skin which breaths and adapts to ventilation requirements.

Als erstes Gebäude neben dem Grundstück, auf dem sich einst die Zwillingstürme erhoben, entsteht ein Hochhaus von 52 Stockwerken, das den Eingang zum Komplex des World Trade Center markiert. Die Fassadenfläche des Turms ist so gestaltet, dass sie wie eine Haut atmet und sich damit in das Lüftungssystem des Gebäudes integriert.

Le bâtiment le plus proche de l'emplacement où se trouvaient les tours jumelles est un gratte-ciel de 52 étages, qui marque l'entrée du complexe du World Trade Center. La surface de la tour a été conçue comme une « peau » qui respire et s'adapte aux besoins de ventilation.

Het eerste gebouw dat oprijst in het gebied direct naast Ground Zero is een wolkenkrabber van 52 verdiepingen die de ingang tot het gebouwencomplex van het World Trade Center markeert. Het oppervlak van de toren is ontworpen als een ademende huid die zich instelt op de behoefte aan ventilatie.

STAY

The Cooper Square Hotel ⑫

25 Cooper Square

Carlos Zapata Studio
www.cz-studio.com

© Wade Zimmeramn

This steel and glass building in The Bowery area is 21 storey high and has 145 rooms. The arrangement of the interior spaces is inspired by the little courtyards in the East Village. Italian designer Antonio Citterio created the interior, and the furnishings are from the company B&B Italia.

Dieser Glas- und Stahlturm im Viertel The Bowery zählt 21 Stockwerke und 145 Zimmer. Die Anordnung der Innenräume ist an die kleinen Höfe des East Villages angelehnt. Für die Innenarchitektur zeichnet der italienische Designer Antonio Citterio verantwortlich; die Möbel stammen von B&B Italia.

Cette tour en acier et en verre située dans la zone de The Bowery comprend 21 étages et 145 chambres. L'organisation des espaces intérieurs est inspirée des petites cours de l'East Village. Le designer italien Antonio Citterio a conçu l'intérieur et les meubles sont de la société B&B Italia.

Deze toren van staal en glas in de wijk The Bowery telt 21 verdiepingen en 145 wooneenheden. De indeling van de ruimten binnen is geïnspireerd op de kleine patio's van East Village. De Italiaanse ontwerper Antonio Citterio verzorgde de binnenhuisarchitectuur en de meubels zijn van B&B Italia.

LEARN

NYU Department of Philosophy (13)

5 Washington Place

Steven Holl Architects
www.stevenholl.com

© Andy Ryan

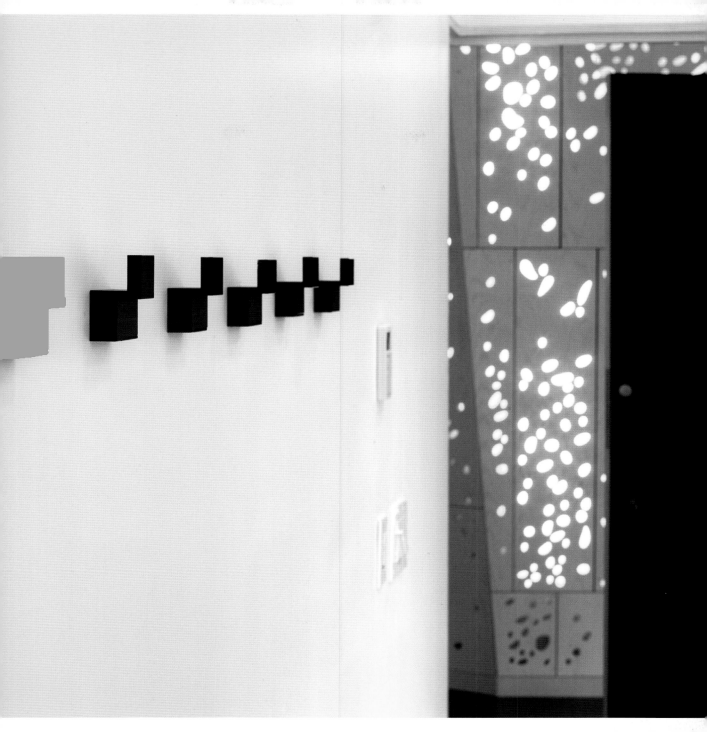

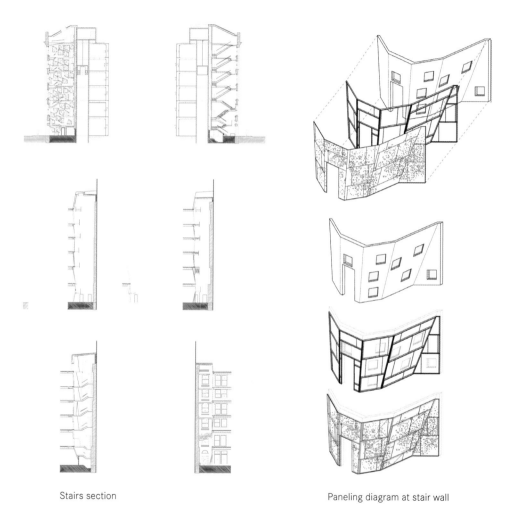

Stairs section

Paneling diagram at stair wall

The remodeling of this building was arranged round the light which floods the six storeys, filtering down the staircase. The handrails and perforated interior walls create light patterns inspired by the book *Remarks on Color* by the philosopher Ludwig Wittgenstein.

Eine entscheidende Rolle beim Umbau dieses Gebäudes spielte das Tageslicht, das über die Treppenhäuser in die sechs Stockwerke strömt. Die Geländer und die durchlässigen Innenwände schaffen Lichtspiele, die von den *Bemerkungen über die Farben* von Ludwig Wittgenstein angeregt wurden.

La rénovation de ce bâtiment est axée sur la lumière qui traverse les six étages et se faufile dans l'escalier. Les balustrades et les murs intérieurs perforés créent des motifs lumineux qui s'inspirent du livre *Remarks on Color* du philosophe Ludwig Wittgenstein.

De renovatie van dit gebouw heeft het licht dat de zes verdiepingen via de trappen binnendringt als uitgangspunt. De balustrades en geperforeerde binnenmuren creëren lichtschakeringen die geïnspireerd zijn op het boek *Remarks on Color* van de filosoof Ludwig Wittgenstein.

LIVE

497 GW Project (14)

497 Greenwich Street

Archi-Tectonics
www.archi-tectonics.com

© Floto & Warner Photography

Rendering

An old 6-storey warehouse was renovated and converted into an 11-storey steel and glass building housing 23 lofts and an art gallery. The folded glass skin on the façade affords a spectacular view of the river.

Ein ehemaliges sechsstöckiges Lagerhaus wurde zu einem elfgeschossigen Gebäude aus Glas und Stahl umgebaut, in dem 23 Lofts und eine Kunstgalerie untergebracht sind. Durch die Fassade aus gefaltetem Glas hat man einen herrlichen Blick auf den Fluss.

Un ancien entrepôt de 6 étages a été rénové et transformé en un bâtiment de 11 étages en acier et en verre, abritant 23 lofts et une galerie d'art. La « peau » en verre plié de la façade donne une vue spectaculaire sur le fleuve.

Dit voormalige pakhuis van zes verdiepingen is door de renovatie veranderd in een gebouw van elf verdiepingen van staal en glas, met daarin 23 lofts en een kunstgalerie. Dankzij de gevel van geplooid glas is er een schitterend uitzicht over het water.

LIVE

Switch Building (15)

109 Norfolk Street

nArchitects
www.narchitects.com

© Frank Oudeman, nArchitects

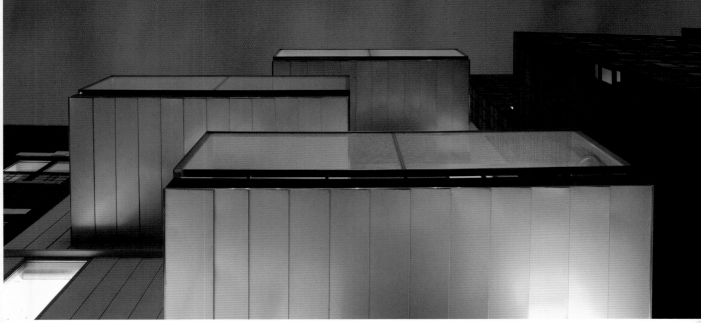

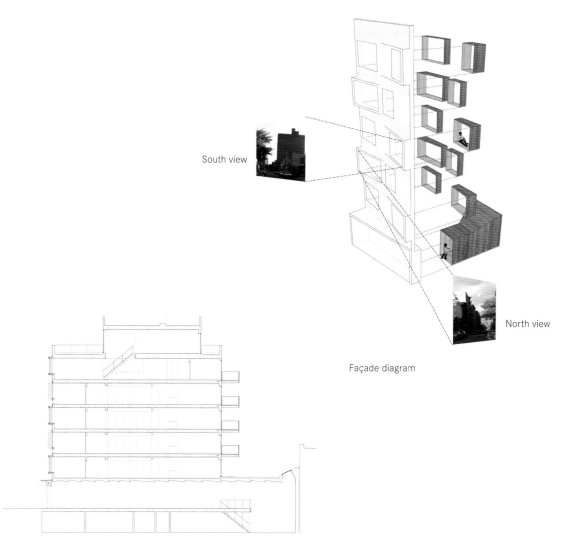

South view

North view

Façade diagram

Section

The façade of this building, which houses homes and an art gallery, is an interpretation of alternating projecting windows, which afford each floor a different view. At the back of the building the apartments are extended by large balconies which, like the façade, create a dynamic effect.

Die Fassade dieses Bauwerks überrascht durch die Neuinterpretation des Fenstererkers. Dadurch offenbart sich von jedem Stockwerk des Gebäudes, in dem Wohnungen und eine Galerie untergebracht sind, ein anderer Blick. Auf der Rückfassade wird durch die großzügigen Balkone ein ähnlich dynamischer Eindruck erzielt.

La façade de cet édifice, qui abrite des habitations et une galerie d'art, est une réinterprétation des fenêtres en saillie en alternance, offrant ainsi une vue différente à chaque étage. Sur la partie arrière, de grands balcons prolongent chacun des appartements ce qui, à l'image de la façade, crée une sensation dynamique.

De gevel van dit gebouw met woningen en een kunstgalerie is een herinterpretatie van de afwisselend uitspringende ramen die elke verdieping een uniek uitzicht bieden. Aan de achterkant hebben alle appartementen grote balkons, die net als de gevel een dynamische aanblik bieden.

SHOP

Marni Mercer Street (16)

159 Mercer Street

Sybarite UK
www.sybarite-uk.com

© Paul Warchol

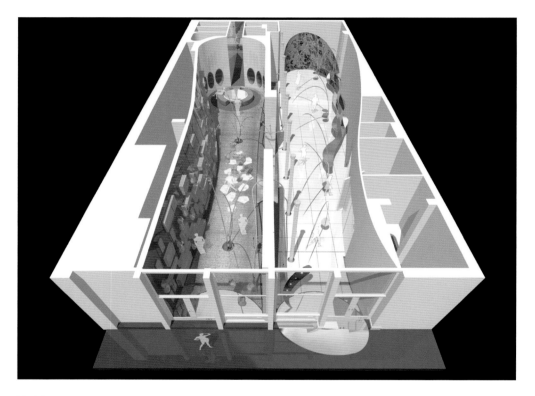

Model

The eclectic style of this boutique reflects the chic, bohemian spirit of Soho. Stainless steel, mirrors and fiberglass make up the various spaces in which this Italian firm displays its different lines of clothing and accessories.

Im uneinheitlichen Erscheinungsbild dieser *Boutique* spiegelt sich der bohèmehafte Chic von Soho wider. Edelstahl, Spiegelglas und Glasfaser sind die Materialien, mit denen die einzelnen Räume zur Darstellung der Modelle und der Accessoires der italienischen Firma gestaltet wurden.

Le style éclectique de cette boutique reflète l'esprit chic et bohème de Soho. De l'acier inoxydable, des miroirs et de la fibre de verre composent plusieurs espaces où sont exposées les différentes lignes de vêtements et d'accessoires de la marque italienne.

De eclectische stijl van deze boetiek weerspiegelt de geest van Soho: bohemien en chic. Roestvrij staal, spiegels en glasvezel scheppen verschillende ruimten waarin diverse kleding- en accessoirelijnen van het Italiaanse merk zijn tentoongesteld.

SHOP

Hugo Boss Store (17)

401 West 14th Street

Matteo Thun
www.matteothun.com

© Paul Warchol

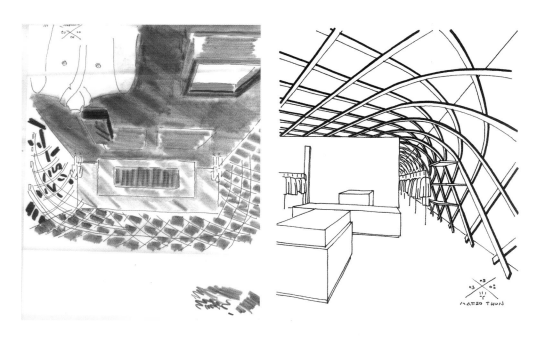

Sketches

In this shop, the first in which all the fashion company's lines have been brought together, the space is defined by a diamond-shaped wooded shell which makes reference to the company's flagship building in Switzerland, also designed by the same architect.

In diesem Geschäft, das erstmals alle Kollektionen des Modehauses vereint, wird der Raum von einer Holzkonstruktion in Diamantenform beherrscht – eine Anspielung auf das Stammhaus in der Schweiz, das vom selben Architekten stammt.

Dans ce magasin, qui rassemble pour la première fois toutes les lignes de l'entreprise de mode, l'espace est délimité par une structure en bois en forme de diamant, qui fait référence au navire amiral du siège de la marque, en Suisse, conçu par le même architecte.

In deze winkel zijn voor het eerst alle lijnen van het modehuis ondergebracht. De ruimte wordt afgegrensd door een houten constructie in de vorm van een diamant, een verwijzing naar het emblematische gebouw van het merk in Zwitserland, dat door dezelfde architect is ontworpen.

SHOP

Droog New York (18)

76 Greene Street

Studio Makkink & Bey
www.jurgenbey.nl

© Isauro Cairo

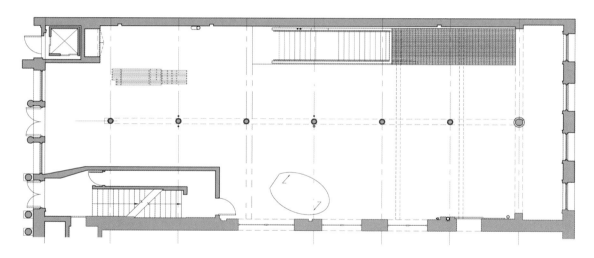

Floor plan

This shop, which belongs to the Dutch designer label, is an atypical and innovative space in line with the philosophy of Droog. It is an installation called *The House of Blue*, made up of elements which can be purchased and delicate pieces from an imaginary house.

Entsprechend der Firmenphilosophie der niederländischen Marke Droog wurde ein eher untypischer, neuartiger Raum geschaffen. Die Installation heißt *The House of Blue* und setzt sich zusammen aus Elementen, die man käuflich erwerben kann, und aus Teilen eines Fantasiehauses.

La boutique de Droog est un espace atypique et novateur, conforme à la philosophie de cette marque hollandaise de design. Elle comporte une installation intitulée "The House of Blue", fabriquée avec des éléments que l'on peut acheter et de délicats éléments d'une maison imaginaire.

De winkel van dit Nederlandse designmerk is een atypische, innovatieve ruimte die past bij de filosofie van Droog. Er is een installatie die *The House of Blue* heet, gemaakt van elementen die te koop zijn en van delicate stukken van een fantasiehuis.

EAT

Charles (19)

234 West Fourth Street

Architecture at Large
www.architectureatlarge.com

© Floto and Warner

Sketch

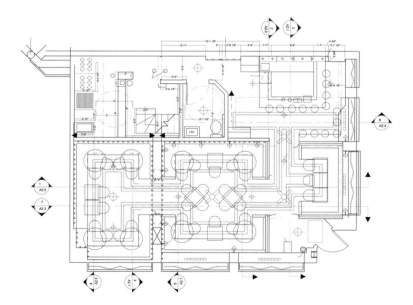

Floor plan

The contrast of dark tones with large mirrors generates an intimate atmosphere in this restaurant, which is characterized by simple shapes and opulent materials that reflect a classical design with contemporary touches.

Durch den Kontrast zwischen den dunklen Tönen und den großflächigen Spiegeln entsteht in diesem Restaurant ein angenehm ruhiges Ambiente. Ansonsten herrschen einfache Formen und ausgewählte Materialien vor. Das Design ist eher klassisch, wenn auch mit einigen zeitgenössischen Details.

Le contraste des tons sombres avec des miroirs de grande taille crée une ambiance intime dans ce restaurant, qui se caractérise par des formes simples et des matériaux opulents qui renvoient à un design classique avec des touches actuelles.

Het contrast tussen donkere kleuren en grote spiegels zorgt voor een intieme sfeer in dit restaurant, dat gekenmerkt wordt door eenvoudige vormen en weelderige materialen. Er wordt met een knipoog naar het heden verwezen naar een klassiek ontwerp.

SHOP

Charlotte Ronson Store [20]

239 Mulberrry Street

Architecture at Large
www.architectureatlarge.com

© Luke Barber Smith

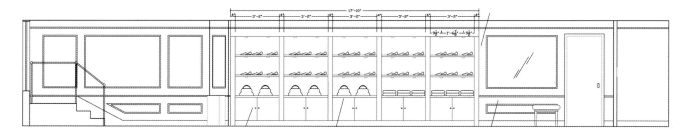

Elevation

The design of this shop tells a story which is more than just the brand. The spaces for the displays all along the central area echo the style of an old boudoir. The details, emphasized by the contrasting paints and the style of decoration, create a chic ambience.

Das Design dieses Ladenlokals verweist weit in die Geschichte zurück. Die Ausstellungsräume im mittleren Bereich erinnern an ein ehemaliges *Boudoir*. Die vielen Details mit ihren Farbkontrasten und der Stil der Dekoration schaffen ein schickes Ambiente.

Le concept de ce magasin renvoie à une histoire qui va au-delà d'une marque. Les espaces d'exposition le long de l'espace central rappellent les anciens boudoirs. Les détails, mis en valeur par les contrastes entre la peinture et le style de la décoration, créent une ambiance chic.

Het ontwerp van deze winkel verwijst naar een geschiedenis die verdergaat dan een merk. De showrooms rondom de centrale ruimte refereren aan een klassiek boudoir. De details, die opvallen dankzij de contrasten in de schildering en de decoratie, zorgen voor een chique sfeer.

SHOP

Wreck Center 21

Temporary Pop up Shop, Soho

Architecture at Large
www.architectureatlarge.com

© Jordan Kleinman

This temporary shop is an installation inspired by the graphics of the 1980s. The walls, floor and areas for displaying products have been almost "bombarded" with spray paint, like subway trains, and decorated with fluorescent adhesive tape.

Diese vorübergehende Ladenausstattung orientiert sich am Grafikdesign der achtziger Jahre. Die Wände, der Boden und die Verkaufsräume sind mit Sprays „verziert" worden, die an die Graffitis auf U-Bahnzügen erinnern. Zusätzlich wurde fluoreszierendes Klebeband verwendet.

Ce magasin temporaire est une installation qui s'inspire du graphisme des années 80. Les murs, le sol et les zones d'exposition des produits ont été tagués avec de la peinture en spray, dans le style des wagons de métro, et décorés avec du ruban adhésif fluorescent.

Deze tijdelijke winkel is een installatie geïnspireerd op de grafische kunst uit de jaren tachtig. De muren, vloer en showrooms zijn bijna 'platgespoten» met spuitbusverf in de stijl van metrotreinstellen en versierd met fluorescerend plakband.

SHOP

Kensiegirl Footwear Showroom ㉒

1370 Avenue of the Americas

Sergio Mannino Studio
www.sergiomannino.com

© Sergio Mannino Studio

In keeping with the style of this brand of women's shoes, this showroom has been designed to be a young, dynamic space, with fluorescent colors and contrasting patterns on the different surfaces.

Gemäß den ästhetischen Vorstellungen des Herstellers von Damenschuhen wurde dieser Verkaufsraum jung und dynamisch gestaltet, mit fluoreszierenden Farben und kontrastreich gemusterten Oberflächen.

Dans la ligne de l'esthétique de la marque de chaussures pour femmes, ce showroom a été conçu comme un espace jeune et dynamique, avec des couleurs fluorescentes et des imprimés contrastés sur les différentes surfaces du lieu.

In overeenstemming met de esthetiek van het merk damesschoenen is deze showroom ontworpen als een frisse, dynamische ruimte, met fluorescerende kleuren en contrasterende prints op de verschillende oppervlakken.

STAY

Smyth (23)

85 West Broadway

BBG-BBGM, Yabu Pushelberg
www.bbg-bbgm.com
www.yabupushelberg.com

© Evan Dion, courtesy of Thompson Hotel

The Tribeca neighborhood forms part of the spirit of this hotel, which has contemporary interiors with touches of classical style. The transparency and open design of this building contrast with the traditional buildings in the area.

Das Lebensgefühl des Viertels Tribeca zeigt sich in den zeitgenössisch ausgestatteten Innenräumen dieses Hotels mit ihrem klassischen Design. Aufgrund seiner Transparenz und Offenheit steht das Gebäude selbst in lebhaftem Kontrast zur traditionellen Bauweise dieser Gegend.

Le quartier de Tribeca suit l'esprit de cet hôtel, qui possède des intérieurs contemporains animés de touches de design classique. Le bâtiment, quant à lui, se démarque des constructions environnantes par sa transparence et son ouverture.

De wijk TriBeCa sluipt de geest van dit hotel binnen via de hedendaagse interieurs die toch iets klassieks hebben. Op zijn beurt contrasteert het gebouw door zijn transparantie en openheid met de traditionele bouwwerken in de omgeving.

LIVE

Posey (24)

East Village

Architecture at Large
www.architectureatlarge.com

© Sophie Munro

The large windows with Parisian-style frames create a romantic air throughout this apartment. The dark materials and the carved wood come alive in spaces which receive so much light.

Durch die Räume dieses Appartements weht ein romantischer Hauch, wie sich etwa bei den großen Fenstern mit ihren Rahmen im Pariser Stil zeigt. Die dunklen, gediegene Materialien und die Holzschnitzereien leben in den hellen Räumen auf.

Une atmosphère romantique emplit cet appartement grâce à des détails comme les grandes fenêtres avec des encadrements de style parisien. Les matériaux de couleur sombre et le bois taillé prennent vie dans les espaces baignés de lumière du jour.

Dankzij details zoals de grote ramen met kozijnen in Parijse stijl heerst een romantische sfeer in de ruimten van dit appartement. De donkere materialen en het houtsnijwerk komen tot leven in ruimten waar veel daglicht binnenvalt.

LIVE

Stam (24)

East Village

Architecture at Large
www.architectureatlarge.com

© Jordan Kleinman

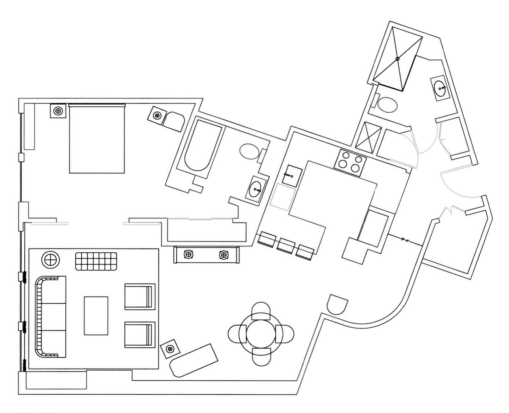

Floor plan

This apartment evokes the golden age of cinema with its rich textiles, golden metals and Art Deco details which combine with vintage style furniture and very feminine colors.

Dieses Appartement erinnert an die goldene Zeit des Kinos: Edle, großzügige Stoffe, Elemente aus goldenem Metall und Art-Déco-Details wurden mit Möbeln im Vintage-Stil und sehr femininen Farben kombiniert.

Cet appartement évoque l'âge d'or du cinéma à partir de riches tissus, de métaux dorés et de détails Art déco combinés avec des meubles de style *vintage* et des couleurs très féminines.

Dit appartement roept de gouden tijd van de film op door zijn rijke stoffen, goudkleurige metalen en art-decodetails in combinatie met vintagemeubelen en heel vrouwelijke kleuren.

LIVE

Greenwich Village Townhouse 26

111 Bedford Street

Axis Mundi
www.axismundi.com

© Andrew Garn, Annie Schlechter

The renovation of this four-storey, neo-Classic house maintained the details and the scale of the original construction while at the same time updating it, making it suitable to house the owner's contemporary art collection.

Beim Umbau dieser viergeschossigen klassizistischen Stadtvilla wurde Wert auf die Details gelegt. Auch das originale Treppenhaus blieb erhalten. Trotzdem ist ein durchaus aktuelles Ambiente entstanden, das der Sammlung zeitgenössischer Kunst des Eigentümers einen angemessenen Rahmen bietet.

La rénovation de cette maison de quatre étages de style néo-classique a respecté les détails et l'échelle de la construction d'origine, tout en l'actualisant et en l'adaptant à la collection d'art contemporain du propriétaire.

Bij de renovatie van deze woning van vier verdiepingen in neoclassicistische stijl zijn de originele details bewaard, evenals de schaal van de oorspronkelijke constructie. Toch is er niet ingeboet aan een actuele context, die nodig was voor de collectie hedendaagse kunst van de eigenaar.

LIVE

Lazzaro Residence 27

505 Grand Street

I-Beam Design
www.i-beamdesign.com

This loft belongs to director and editor Glenn Lazzaro, and is the result of the renovation of an old apartment. The new open, minimalist design is the perfect backdrop for the owner's collection of Eames furniture.

Das Loft gehört dem Regisseur und Produzent Glenn Lazzaro und entstand als Ergebnis des Umbaus eines alten Appartements. Durch die neue Gestaltung kommt die Möbelsammlung des Eigentümers mit Stücken von Charles Eames besonders gut zur Geltung.

Ce loft, propriété du réalisateur et éditeur Glenn Lazzaro, est le résultat de la rénovation d'un ancien appartement. Le nouveau design ouvert et minimaliste fait ressortir la collection de meubles d'Eames du propriétaire.

Deze loft van directeur/uitgever Glenn Lazzaro is het resultaat van de renovatie van een oud appartement. In het nieuwe, open, minimalistische ontwerp komt de collectie Eames-meubels van de eigenaar goed uit de verf.

LIVE

Duane Street Live/Work Loft ㉘ and Garden

132 Duane Street

Marpillero Pollak Architects
www.mparchitectsnyc.com

© Jeff Goldberg/ESTO

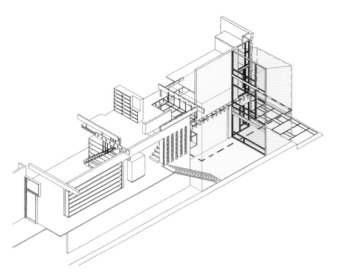

Diagram substracting

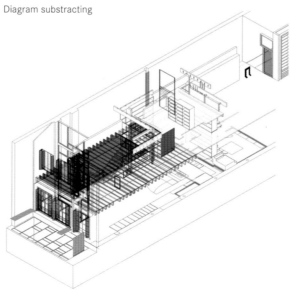

Diagram recycling

Architects converted an old 19th century industrial building to create this loft. The basement of the original structure was transformed into a bright, vital space with mezzanines, open to a garden through a glazed wall.

Dieses Loft entstand in Folge des Umbaus eines ehemaligen Industriegebäudes des 19. Jhs. Das Untergeschoss des Altbaus wurde in einen hellen Wohnraum mit Zwischendecken verwandelt, der sich über eine gläserne Wand zu einem Garten hin öffnet.

Ce loft est le résultat de l'intervention des architectes sur un ancien édifice industriel du XIXe siècle. Le sous-sol de la structure d'origine est devenu un lieu de vie lumineux avec des mezzanines s'ouvrant sur un jardin par une baie vitrée.

Deze loft is het resultaat van een architectonische ingreep in een voormalig industrieel gebouw uit de 19e eeuw. Het souterrain van de oorspronkelijke structuur werd veranderd in een lichte, levendige ruimte met tussenverdiepingen die via een glazen wand uitziet op een tuin.

PLAY

Imagination Playground 29

South Street Seaport Area

Rockwell Group
www.rockwellgroup.com

Renderings: © Kinnaresh Mistry and Rockwell Group

This park will be installed in an area which has grown 35% in the last decade, resulting in more than 15,000 new apartments for families with children. The design incorporates maritime elements inspired by the surroundings.

Die Einwohnerzahl des Stadtteils, in dem dieser Park entstehen soll, ist in den letzten zehn Jahren um rund 35% gestiegen. Es sind über 15.000 neue Wohnungen für Familien mit Kindern entstanden. Bei der Gestaltung des Parks fließen auch Anregungen von der nahen Meersküste ein.

Ce parc sera installé dans une zone qui a vu sa population augmenter de 35 % au cours des dix dernières années, ce qui a impliqué la construction de plus de 15 000 appartements neufs pour des familles avec des enfants. Son design inclut des éléments marins qui s'inspirent de l'environnement.

Dit park zal worden aangelegd in een gebied waarvan de bevolking de laatste tien jaar met 35 procent gegroeid is. Die toename heeft geleid tot meer dan 15000 nieuwe appartementen voor gezinnen met kinderen. In het ontwerp zijn op de omgeving geïnspireerde mariene elementen opgenomen.

SEE

New Amsterdam Plein & Pavilion (30)

The Battery

UNStudio
www.unstudio.com

© Richard Koek
Drawings: © UNStudio

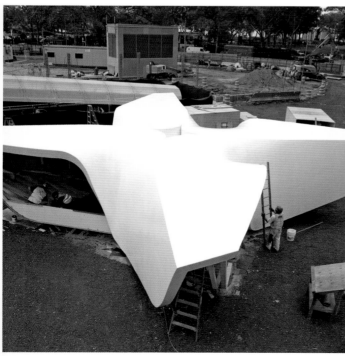

This meeting place in Battery Park will mark the 400th anniversary of Henry Hudson's arrival in New York. The focal point will be a flower-shaped pavilion which, at night, will change color through the use of an LED illumination system on the façade.

An diesem Treffpunkt im Battery Park wird das 400jährige Jubiläum der Ankunft Henry Hudsons in New York gefeiert werden. Im Mittelpunkt soll ein Pavillon in Blumenform stehen, der nachts dank LED-Leuchten in der Fassade seine Farbe ändern kann.

Ce lieu de rencontre dans le Battery Park célèbrera le 400e anniversaire de l'arrivée d'Henry Hudson à New York. Un pavillon en forme de fleur, qui changera de couleur la nuit grâce à un système d'éclairage à base de leds sur la façade, tiendra la vedette.

Met deze ontmoetingsruimte in Battery Park zal gevierd worden dat Henry Hudson 400 jaar geleden in New York aankwam. Een bloemvormig paviljoen dat 's avonds voortdurend van kleur verandert dankzij een led-verlichtingssysteem in de gevel, is de grote blikvanger.

STROLL

The Battery Bosque and SeaGlass (31)

Battery Park

WXY Architecture
www.wxystudio.com

© Amy Barkow
Drawings and renderings: © WXY Architecture

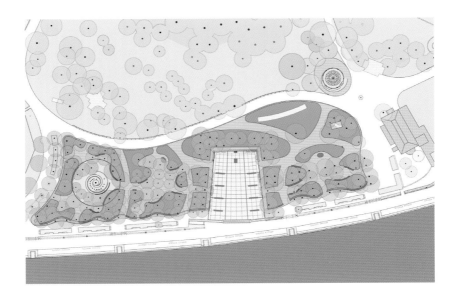

Site plan

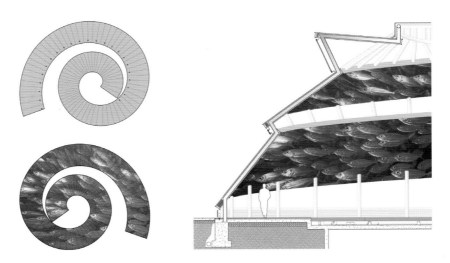

Partial section

What used to be an area of almost 97,000 sq ft of asphalt is being transformed into a park with an abundance of plant life and installations made of wood from responsibly-managed forests. A spiral-shaped carousel with an interior screen on which maritime subjects can be projected will complete the final stage of the creation of this new lung for New York.

Wo sich zuvor eine fast 9.000 m^2 große Asphaltfläche befand, liegt heute ein Park mit ausgedehnten Grünanlagen und Holzmöbeln aus kontrolliertem Einschlag. Ein spiralförmiges Karussell mit einer Leinwand, auf die Szenen vom Meeresleben projiziert werden, schließt die letzte Umbauphase dieser neuen grünen Lunge New Yorks ab.

À l'endroit où se trouvait auparavant une zone de quasiment 9 000 m^2 d'asphalte, on trouve désormais un parc doté d'installations fabriquées avec du bois provenant de forêts contrôlées. Un carrousel en forme de spirale avec un écran intérieur sur lequel sont projetés des thèmes marins marquera l'achèvement de la dernière étape d'aménagement de ce nouveau « poumon » new-yorkais.

Waar eerst bijna 9000 m^2 aan asfalt was, ligt nu een park met een overvloed aan natuur en voorzieningen van hout uit gecontroleerde bossen. Een spiraalvormige carrousel met binnenin een scherm waarop beelden van de zee worden geprojecteerd, zal de laatste fase vormen van de herinrichting van deze nieuwe groene long.

REMEMBER

Irish Hunger Memorial (32)

290 Vesey Street

1100 Architect
www.1100architect.com

© Peter Aaron/ESTO

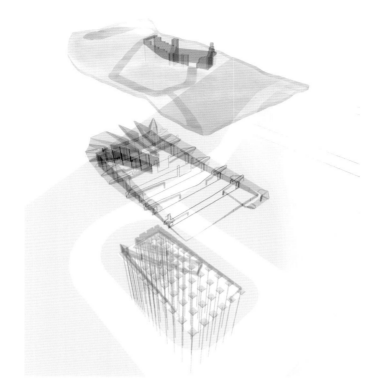

Structural diagram

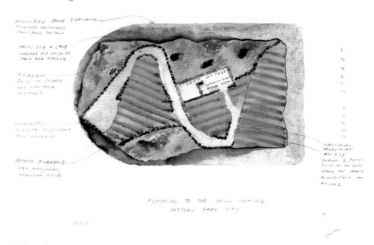

Watercolor

Many of the people who fled the famine that gripped Ireland in the 19th century went to the United States, and this urban installation in southern Manhattan was erected in their memory. On a base of stone and glass, the Irish landscape has been recreated with native plants which make up a live monument that continues to evolve.

Die Vereinigten Staaten waren bevorzugtes Auswanderungsziel der Menschen, die Irland während der großen Hungersnot des 19. Jhs. verließen. An dieses historische Ereignis erinnert diese Installation im Süden Manhattans: Auf einem Sockel aus Glas und Stein wurde die irische Landschaft mit den dort heimischen Pflanzen nachempfunden und so ein lebendiges, sich ständig veränderndes Denkmal geschaffen.

Cette installation urbaine au sud de Manhattan a été érigée en souvenir des nombreuses personnes ayant fui la grande famine qui a ravagé l'Irlande au XIXe siècle. Sur une base en pierre et en verre, le paysage irlandais a été recréé avec des plantes indigènes, qui composent un monument vivant en constante évolution.

De VS vormden de bestemming van veel Ieren die hun land ontvluchtten tijdens de grote hongersnood in de 19e eeuw. Als gedenkteken werd deze installatie in het zuiden van Manhattan gebouwd. Met steen en glas is het Ierse landschap nagebootst, met inheemse planten die een levend, zich ontwikkelend monument vormen.

MIDTOWN

9th Ave

Central Park St

2

7th Ave

9 14

Madison Ave

59th St

7

6

6th Ave

20

22

23

21

25

19

5th Ave

Park Ave

5

15

1

28

Times
Square

Hell´s
Kitchen

42nd St

39th St

34th St

13

Grand
Terminal
Central

Sutton
Place

24

12

42nd St

3

39th St

2nd Ave

18

Chelsea

34th St

Murray
Hill

1st Ave

12th Ave

10th Ave

6th Ave

8th Ave

7th Ave

5th Ave

Madison Ave

4

29

16

17

26

Madison
Square
Park

Park Ave

Gramercy
Park

14th St

6th Ave

7

11

27

Flatiron
District

Union
Square Park

10

2nd Ave

14th St

WORK

The New York Times Building (1)

620 Eighth Avenue

Renzo Piano Building Workshop, Fox & Fowle Architects
http://rpbw.r.ui-pro.com
www.fxfowle.com

© Michel Denancé

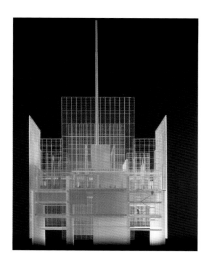

Schematic desing. Detail of the
model with the roof garden

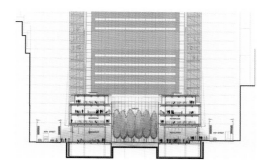

Development design. Cross section
through podium garden

South elevation

This steel and glass building reinforces this famous New York newspaper's ideal of transparency. An exterior drape with ceramic bars filters the sunlight. The bright lobby and the impressive interior garden can been seen from the street.

Glas und Stahl stehen sinnbildlich für die Stärke und Offenheit der berühmten New Yorker Zeitung. Ein Vorhang aus Keramikstäben schützt vor der direkten Sonneneinstrahlung. Schon von der Straße aus sind die helle *Lobby* und der eindrucksvolle Gartenhof zu erkennen.

Ce bâtiment en acier et en verre accentue l'idéal de transparence de ce célèbre journal new-yorkais. Un rideau extérieur avec des tiges en céramique sert de filtre solaire. De la rue, on aperçoit le lobby lumineux et l'impressionnant jardin intérieur.

Het gebouw van staal en glas versterkt het ideaal van transparantie van deze beroemde New Yorkse krant. Aan de buitenkant werkt een scherm met aardewerken staafjes als een zonnefilter. Vanaf de straat zijn de lichte lobby en de indrukwekkende binnentuin zichtbaar.

WORK

Hearst Corporation Headquarters ②

300 West 57th Street

Foster and Partners
www.fosterandpartners.com
© Nigel Young/Foster and Partners

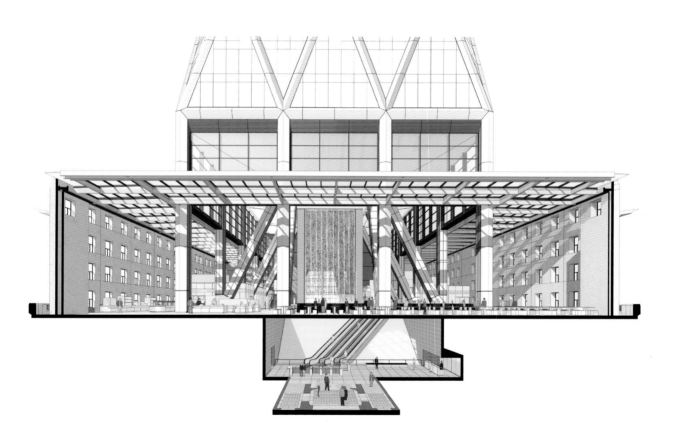

Section

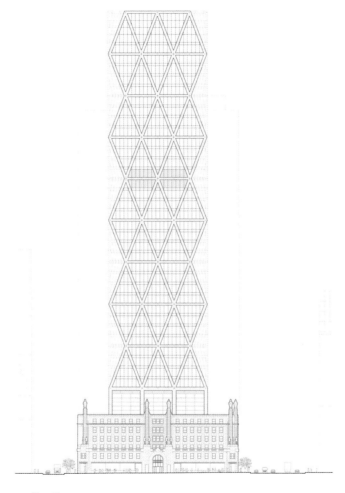

Elevation

This new 42-storey structure, on a 1928 Art Deco building, has been constructed following guidelines for sustainability. 85% of the steel employed is recycled and the building uses 26% less energy than conventional ones.

Das neue 42stöckige Turmhochhaus wurde über einem Art-Déco-Gebäude von 1928 errichtet. Dem Prinzip der Nachhaltigkeit folgend wurde zu 85% wiederverwerteter Stahl verwendet und der Energieverbrauch um ein Viertel reduziert.

Cette nouvelle tour de 42 étages sur le bâtiment Art déco de 1928 a été construite selon des directives de développement durable. C'est ainsi que 85 % de l'acier utilisé est recyclable et qu'elle consomme 26 % d'énergie en moins que les édifices traditionnels.

Bij de bouw van de nieuwe toren van 42 verdiepingen boven op het art-decogebouw uit 1928 zijn richtlijnen van duurzaamheid gevolgd. Zo is 85 procent van het gebruikte staal gerecycled en gebruikt het gebouw 26 procent minder energie dan traditionele gebouwen.

WORK

Bofa Tower at One Bryant Park ③

One Bryant Park

Cook + Fox Architects
www.cookplusfox.com

© Wade Zimmerman

This steel, aluminum and glass skyscraper houses the Bank of America. In addition to its innovative design it also incorporates environmentally friendly technology. The most obvious example is the external glass drape, which allows light in and affords views of the surroundings, but protects against the heat.

In diesem Wolkenkratzer aus Stahl, Aluminium und Glas sind die Büroräume der Bank of America untergebracht. Innovatives Design wird hier mit modernster Umwelttechnik verbunden. Am besten wird dies am äußeren Glasvorhang deutlich, der das Tageslicht einlässt und weite Ausblicke erlaubt, während er zugleich gegen Wärme isoliert.

Ce gratte-ciel en acier, en aluminium et en verre abrite les bureaux de la Bank of America. À son design novateur s'ajoute une technologie respectueuse de l'environnement. L'exemple le plus évident en est le rideau en verre extérieur, qui permet à la lumière d'entrer et optimise les vues, tout en protégeant de la chaleur.

Deze wolkenkrabber van staal, aluminium en glas huisvest de Bank of America. Het innovatieve ontwerp is gaat samen met milieuvriendelijke technologie. Het opvallendst is het glazen scherm aan de buitenkant. Het laat het daglicht door en zorgt voor maximaal uitzicht, terwijl het de warmte tegenhoudt.

WORK

The IAC Building ④

529-555 West 18th Street

Gehry Partners
www.foga.com

© IAC

The first building by architect Frank Gehry in New York houses the offices of IAC, a company specializing in communication services. The structure was built to look like a glass boat sailing on Manhattan Island. The transparent façades are transformed at night by spectacular illumination.

Das erste Bauwerk der Architekten Frank Gehry in New York beherbergt die Geschäftsräume des auf Kommunikation spezialisierten Unternehmens IAC. Der Bau scheint wie ein gläsernes Schiff über die Insel Manhattan zu gleiten. Nachts ziehen die raffiniert erleuchteten Fassaden alle Blicke an.

Le premier bâtiment de l'architecte Frank Gehry à New York abrite les bureaux de la société IAC, spécialisée dans des services de communication. La structure ressemble à un bateau en verre qui navigue dans l'île de Manhattan. Ses façades transparentes se transforment la nuit grâce à un éclairage spectaculaire.

Dit gebouw in New York van architect Frank Gehry huisvest de kantoren van IAC, een bedrijf in internet services & retailing. Het bouwwerk is als een glazen schip dat over het eiland Manhattan vaart. De transparante gevels ondergaan 's avonds dankzij spectaculaire verlichting een totale metamorfose.

STAY & LIVE

Cassa (5)

45th Street between Fifth and Sixth

Ten Arquitectos
www.ten-arquitectos.com

Renderings: © Ten Arquitectos

Cassa, a condominium hotel which will contain 57 homes and 166 rooms, is to be added to the New York skyline. The façade of the building will be a surface with perforations for the windows, which maintains its own rhythm across the length and breadth of the building.

Cassa, ein Hotel und Appartementhaus, wird bald die *Skyline* New Yorks bereichern. Der Komplex umfasst 57 Eigentumswohnungen und 166 Hotelzimmer. Die Fassade stellt sich wie eine nach einem festgelegten Prinzip rhythmisch von Fenstern durchlöcherte Fläche dar.

Cassa, un hôtel en copropriété qui contiendra 57 suites et 166 chambres, s'ajoutera au *skyline* de New York. La façade de l'édifice se présentera comme une surface perforée par les fenêtres, qui conservent un rythme particulier tout au long du bâtiment.

Cassa, een condominiumhotel, zal met zijn 57 woningen en 166 kamers worden toegevoegd aan de skyline van New York. In de gevel van het gebouw zullen de ramen in een bijzonder patroon het oppervlak lijken te perforeren, zowel over de lengte als de breedte.

SHOP

Louis Vuitton New York ⑥

1 East 57th Street

Jun Aoki & Associates
www.aokijun.com

© Dan Bibb

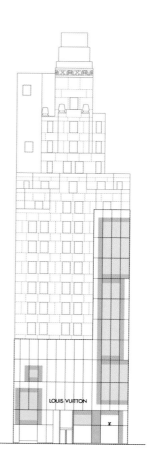

Elevations

Jun Aoki designed the façade of this building with a finish comprising two superimposed glass sheets. The interior layer is engraved with Louis Vuitton's distinctive logo, and the other layer alternates between opaque and transparent.

Jun Aoki hat die Fassade dieses Gebäudes mit ihrer Doppelglasschale entworfen. Die innere Schicht trägt das typische Grundmuster der Erzeugnisse von Louis Vuitton, während sich in der zweiten transparente und opake Flächen abwechseln.

Jun Aoki a conçu la façade de ce bâtiment dont la finition est formée de deux vitrines superposées. La partie intérieure porte le logo distinctif de Louis Vuitton et l'autre alterne entre opacité et transparence.

Jun Aoki heeft de gevel van dit gebouw ontworpen: een afwerking van twee tegen elkaar geplaatste glazen platen. Op de binnenste laag is het kenmerkende beeldmerk van Louis Vuitton gegraveerd. In de tweede laag worden doorzichtigheid en matheid afgewisseld.

LIVE

Avant Chelsea ⑦

245 West 19th Street

1100 Architect
www.1100architect.com

© Eduard Hueber

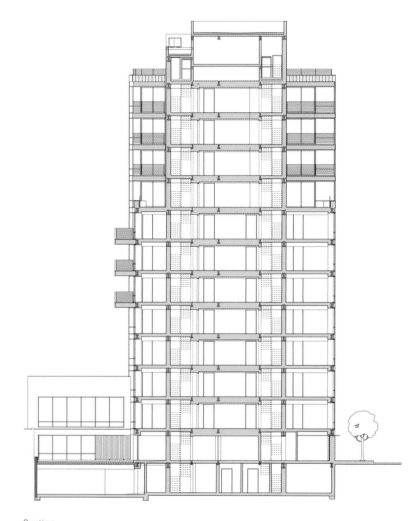

Section

This 12 storey building opens gradually to the light and air through terraces in a staggered formation on the upper part of the building. One of the walls is clad in a mosaic of 2,500 pieces in different tones of indigo, making the construction stand out from its surroundings.

Das zwölfstöckige Gebäude erschließt sich über die im oberen Teil stufenartig angeordneten Terrassen dem Tageslicht und der frischen Luft. Der Bau sticht in der Umgebung hervor durch seine Wandverkleidung, die sich aus 2.500 Mosaikteilchen in den verschiedensten Blautönen zusammensetzt.

Cette tour de 12 étages s'ouvre progressivement à la lumière et à l'air par les terrasses qui s'échelonnent sur la partie supérieure du bâtiment. La construction se distingue de son environnement par un de ses murs recouverts d'une mosaïque de 2 500 panneaux dans différents tons d'indigo.

Via de opeenvolgende terrassen in het bovenste gedeelte van het gebouw krijgt deze twaalf verdiepingen hoge toren geleidelijk uitzicht op licht en lucht. Het bouwwerk springt eruit dankzij een van de muren, die bekleed is met een mozaïek van 2500 panelen in verschillende indigotinten.

SHOP

Armani Fifth Avenue (8)

717 Fifth Avenue

Doriana & Massimiliano Fuksas
www.fuksas.it

© Ramon Prat, courtesy of Fuksas

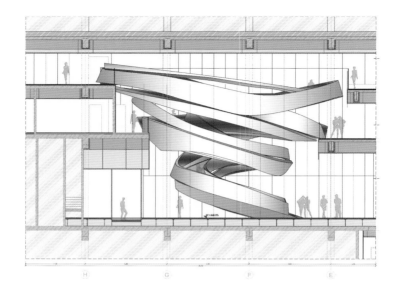

Main stair elevation

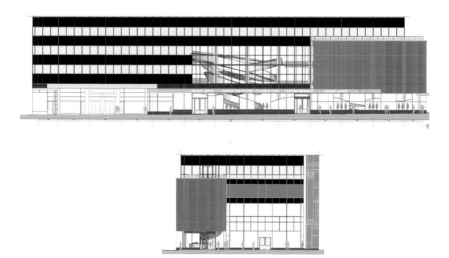

Elevations

Designed as a unique space, the different levels of the shop appear connected by the center of the spectacular staircase. Its dynamic structure makes it an undeniable focal point and enhances the fluidity and movement which characterize the design of the premises.

Die verschiedenen Ebenen des Ladenlokals werden untereinander durch den Spiralwirbel der Aufsehen erregenden Treppe verbunden. Aufgrund ihrer dynamischen Struktur ist sie der absolute Blickpunkt des Ladens und verleiht dem Design eine fließende Bewegung.

Cette boutique est conçue comme un espace unique, et les différents niveaux de la boutique semblent connectés par la partie centrale d'un escalier spectaculaire. Sa structure dynamique améliore la fluidité et le mouvement qui caractérisent le design de ce lieu.

De in één enkele ruimte ondergebrachte niveaus van de winkel lijken met elkaar verbonden te worden door de werveling van de spectaculaire trap. Door zijn dynamische structuur is de trap de absolute blikvanger en versterkt hij de beweeglijke vloeiendheid die kenmerkend is voor het ontwerp van dit pand.

EAT

Nobu Fifty Seven ⑨

40 West 57th Street

Rockwell Group
www.rockwellgroup.com

© Scott Frances

Sketch

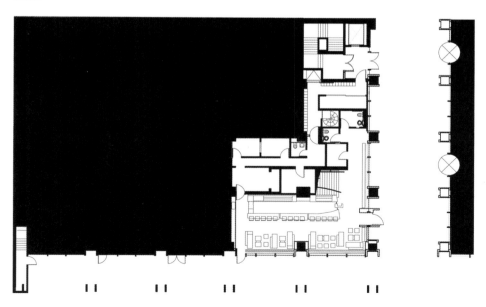

Floor plan

The first Nobu restaurant was based on the innovative cuisine of chef Nobu Matsuhisa and on Japanese culture. With Nobu Fifty Seven the architects were inspired by the Japanese landscape and its connections with the sea, and so water and waves are the predominant themes in this dynamic space.

Das erste Nobu Restaurant bietet die neuartige Küche des *Chefs* Nobu Matsuhisa und echt japanische Esskultur. Bei der Einrichtung des Nobu Fifty Seven haben sich die Innenarchitekten von der japanischen Landschaft und ihrer engen Verbindung zum Meer inspirieren lassen. Das Wasser und seine wogenden Bewegungen verleihen dem Raum seine Dynamik.

Le premier restaurant Nobu est basé sur la cuisine novatrice du chef Nobu Matsuhisa et sur la culture nipponne. Pour Nobu Fifty Seven, les architectes se sont inspirés du paysage japonais et de ses liens avec la mer. L'eau et ses mouvements d'ondulation sont le thème dominant dans cet espace dynamique.

Het eerste Nobu-restaurant heeft de innovatieve keuken van chef-kok Nobu Matsuhisa en de Japanse cultuur als basis. Voor Nobu Fifty Seven hebben de architecten zich laten inspireren door het Japanse landschap en zijn verbinding met de zee. Het hoofdthema in deze dynamische ruimte is (golvend) water.

EAT

Wildwood BBQ 10

225 Park Avenue South

Rockwell Group
www.rockwellgroup.com

© Eric Laignel

-ALL·DAY-
~STARTERS~

Kicked·Up Caesar
Honey Cornbread Croutons, Creamy Chipotle Dressing

Jailhouse Red Chili
Smoked Brisket, Pinto Beans

Chicken Wings
-Rubbed & Fried-
OR
-Slathered-
with
·Chipotle·Raspberry·

Frank's Redhot

Bottle Caps
Beer-Battered Fried Jalapeña Slices, Ranch Dressing

The Hutto Texas Wedge
Iceberg, Candied Pecans, Bacon, Blue Cheese Dressing

This 3,500 sq ft space brings together rustic and industrial styles. The former is evident in the wooden roof and the latter is visible in the steel garage door with nicotine stained glass panels and the original cement floor.

Auf 325 m² verschmelzen rustikale und industrielle Ästhetik miteinander. Während das ländliche Element sich vor allem in der Holzdecke ausdrückt, zeigt sich das industrielle Erbe an den Garagentüren aus Stahl mit ihren gerauchten Glasscheiben und am noch original erhaltenen Zementboden.

Dans cet espace de 325 m², l'esthétique rustique se fond avec le style industriel. Tandis que la première se manifeste dans le toit en bois, le second est visible dans les portes en acier du garage dotées de panneaux en verre teint et le sol d'origine en ciment.

In deze ruimte van 325 m² vermengen rustieke en industriële esthetiek zich met elkaar. Terwijl het rustieke zich laat zien in het houten dak, is het industriële zichtbaar in de stalen garagedeuren met rookglazen panelen en de oorspronkelijke cementen vloer.

SHOP

M·A·C Pro Store (11)

7 West 22nd Street

M·A·C in House Design
www.maccosmetics.com

© Visual ID Lab

This store, belonging to the famous cosmetics firm, is made up of two spaces: the first is for selling products and is also equipped with make-up points for clients, and the other, which is for training staff, is like a laboratory with a large sink and jars of pigments.

Das Ladenlokal der berühmten Kosmetikfirma umfasst zwei Bereiche: Einer ist für den Verkauf der Produkte bestimmt und verfügt über individuelle Schminkstände für die Kundinnen, der andere dient als Trainingslabor für die Kosmetikerinnen und ist mit einem großen Becken und Farbproben ausgestattet.

Cette boutique de la célèbre société de cosmétiques se compose de deux espaces : l'un pour la vente de produits, équipé de postes de maquillage pour les clients, et l'autre pour le divertissement des maquilleurs qui contient, tel un laboratoire, un grand évier et des bocaux de pigments.

Dit pand van het beroemde cosmeticamerk bevat twee ruimten. De ene is bestemd voor de verkoop van producten en is uitgerust met stands waar cliënten kunnen worden opgemaakt. In de andere, waar als in een laboratorium allerlei gekleurde flesjes en potjes staan, worden visagistes opgeleid.

SHOP

Gokaldas 12

1400 Broadway

I-Beam Design
www.i-beamdesign.com

© Filian Mattisch

The objective of this project was to create a flexible, open space in which to present different collections of clothes. The pure white which dominates on all the resin surfaces makes the garments look as if they are floating in the air.

Bei diesem Projekt ging es darum, einen offenen, flexibel zu gestaltenden Ausstellungsraum für die verschiedenen Modekollektionen zu schaffen. Das auf allen Kunstharzoberflächen vorherrschende reine Weiß lässt die einzelnen Stücke fast im Raum schweben.

Ce projet avait pour objectif de créer un espace pratique et ouvert pour présenter les différentes collections de vêtements. Le blanc absolu, qui prédomine dans toutes les surfaces en résine, donne l'impression que les vêtements flottent dans l'air.

Dit ontwerp had tot doel een flexibele, open ruimte te creëren voor de presentatie van diverse kledingcollecties. Door het wit, dat alle oppervlakken van hars volledig domineert, lijken de kledingstukken in de ruimte te zweven.

SHOP

Fila New York ⑬

340 Madison Avenue

Giorgio Borruso Design
www.borrusodesign.com

© Benny Chan / Fotoworks

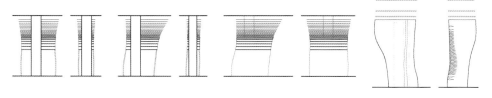

Metal column sections

Air curtain elevations

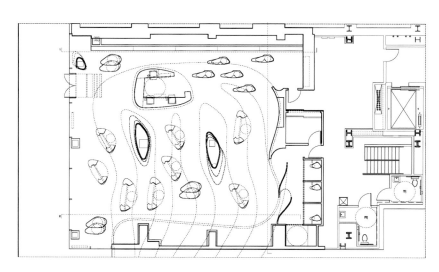

Floor plan

The furnishings in this shop, which belongs to an Italian sports clothing company, look like the tensed muscles of an athlete. As with the curved, sinuous lines and the reflections which dominate the space, all the elements in the property are inspired by sport.

Das Mobiliar der Verkaufsräume dieses italienischen Sportkleidungsherstellers erinnert an die gespannten Muskeln eines Athleten. Runde, geschwungene Linien, Reflexe und alle anderen Elemente in diesem Raum schaffen einen unmittelbaren Bezug zum Sport.

Le mobilier de ce magasin, qui appartient à une marque italienne de vêtements de sport, rappelle les muscles tendus de l'athlète. Tout comme les lignes courbes et sinueuses et les reflets qui dominent l'espace, l'ensemble des éléments de ce lieu est inspiré du monde du sport.

Het meubilair in de winkel van dit Italiaanse sportkledingmerk doet denken aan de aangespannen spieren van een atleet. Niet alleen de gebogen, kronkelende lijnen en de weerspiegelingen die de ruimte overheersen, maar alle elementen in dit pand zijn geïnspireerd op sport.

WORK

Louis Vuitton New York Offices and Showroom (14)

1 East 57th Street

ikon.5 architects
www.ikon5architects.com

© James D'Addio

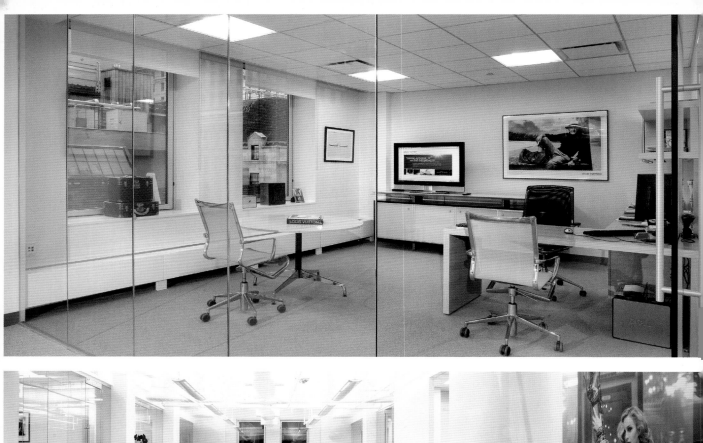

The renovation of the offices in Louis Vuitton's flagship store resulted in a minimalist, neutral style with bright spaces and fine materials inspired by the textures and colors of this French fashion label.

Die Erneuerung der Büroräume im *Flagship store* der Firma Louis Vuitton fand im Zeichen einer neutralen, minimalistischen Ästhetik statt. Geschaffen wurden sehr helle Räume aus edlen Materialien, deren Farben und Oberflächen an den Produkten des französischen Modehauses orientiert sind.

La rénovation des bureaux installés dans le navire amiral de Louis Vuitton a intégré une esthétique minimaliste et neutre, avec des ambiances lumineuses et des matériaux nobles inspirés des textures et des couleurs de la marque de luxe française.

Bij de renovatie van de kantoren in de *flagship store* van Louis Vuitton werd een minimalistische, neutrale esthetiek ingevoerd: heel lichte ruimten en mooie materialen, die zijn geïnspireerd op de materialen en kleuren van het Franse modemerk.

SHOP

Pronovias (15)

14 East 52nd Street

GCA Arquitectes Associats

© Jordi Miralles, Wade Zimmerman

FROM BARCELONA
TO NEW YORK

PRONOVIAS

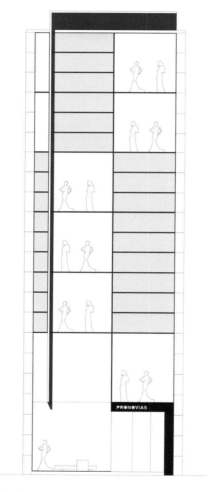

Section

The glass façade turns the building into a light box which serves as an advertisement for this wedding wear label. Comprising more than 22,600 sq ft over 9 floors, there are spaces for showrooms, private fashion shows and offices.

Die verglaste Fassade verwandelt das Gebäude in einen Kasten aus Licht, der gleichsam als Reklame für das Brautmodenhaus fungiert. In neun Stockwerken mit über 2.100 Quadratmetern ist genug Platz für Ausstellung, private Vorführräume und Büros.

La façade vitrée transforme le bâtiment en une boîte lumineuse, qui sert de publicité à cette marque de vêtements de mariage. Les plus de 2 100 mètres carrés répartis sur 9 étages comprennent des espaces pour des *showrooms*, des défilés privés et des bureaux.

Het vele glas van de gevel maakt het gebouw tot een soort doos van licht die dienstdoet als een advertentie voor het bruidsmodemerk zelf. Op de negen verdiepingen van samen meer dan 2100 m² aan oppervlakte zijn showrooms, kantoren en ruimten voor privémodeshows.

EAT

llili **16**

236 Fifth Avenue

Nasser Nakib Architect
www.nassernakib.com

© Chris Goodney

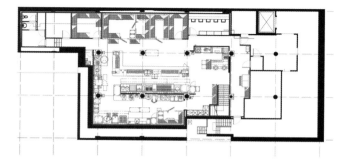

Cellar plan

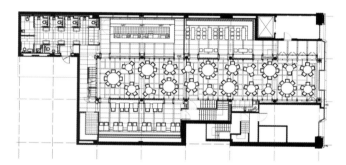

Ground floor plan

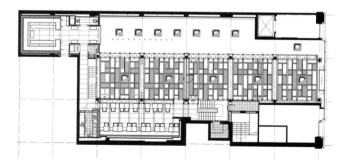

Mezzanine plan

Inspired by the spirit of Lebanon, this restaurant is located in contemporary surroundings. Although the areas can be distinguished from each other by their architecture, they are unified by a design with pure lines, warm textiles, gentle lighting and provocative combinations.

Trotz der modernen Umgebung liegen die Wurzeln dieses Restaurants im Libanon. Die einzelnen Bereiche sind zwar architektonisch voneinander differenziert, finden aber dank des gradlinigen Designs, der warmen Stoffe, der angenehmen Beleuchtung und der überraschenden Kombinationen zu einem einheitlichen Gesamteindruck zusammen.

Ce restaurant, qui s'inspire de l'esprit du Liban, est situé dans un environnement contemporain. Bien que les différents espaces se distinguent architecturalement les uns des autres, ils sont unifiés par un design aux lignes pures, des tissus chaleureux, un éclairage doux et des combinaisons audacieuses.

Dit restaurant is geïnspireerd op de Libanese geest en staat in een hedendaagse omgeving. Hoewel de gebieden zich architectonisch gezien van elkaar onderscheiden, vormen ze een eenheid door een ontwerp van zuivere lijnen, warme stoffen, suggestieve verlichting en gedurfde combinaties.

CHILL OUT

1 OAK 17

435 West 17th Street

Roy Nachum
www.roynachum.com

© Adam Friedberg

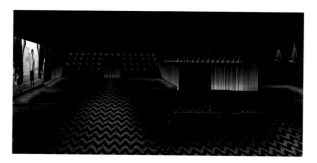

Renderings

This exclusive lounge in Chelsea has an eclectic interior with retro furnishings from different decades, all brought together by a range of warm tones. Particularly eye-catching are the wall made of 10,000 wooden letters and the Brazilian oak bar which looks like an enormous piano.

Diese exklusive *Lounge* in Chelsea offenbart ein Sammelsurium an Nostalgiemöbeln, das aber durch die warmen Farbnuancen doch einheitlich wirkt. Hervorzuheben sind auch die Wand aus 10.000 hölzernen Buchstaben und die Bar aus brasilianischer Eiche in Form eines riesenhaften Klaviers.

Ce lounge huppé de Chelsea présente un intérieur éclectique, avec un mobilier rétro d'époques différentes mais unifié par une gamme de tons chaleureux. Le mur composé de 10 000 lettres en bois ainsi que la barre en chêne brésilien qui ressemble à un énorme piano attirent immédiatement l'attention.

Deze exclusieve lounge in Chelsea toont een eclectisch interieur met retromeubilair uit verschillende decennia, dat echter een eenheid vormt door het gamma van warme tinten. Opvallend zijn de muur van tienduizend houten letters en de bar van Braziliaans eiken die op een enorme piano lijkt.

STAY

Ace Hotel 18

20 West 29th Street

Roman & Williams
www.romanandwilliams.com

© Ace Hotel

The Ace occupies the old Breslin Hotel in a building constructed in 1908; as with other properties in the vicinity, the changes in the neighborhood marked the end of an era of glory. But the area which today is known as NoMad (North of Madison Square) is currently undergoing a revival which is reflected in the eclectic decoration of the hotel.

Das Ace Hotel ist im Gebäude des ehemaligen Breslin von 1908 untergebracht. Dieses und die benachbarten Gebäude schienen ihre beste Zeit schon hinter sich zu haben. Doch das als NoMad (North of Madison Square) bekannt gewordene Viertel erlebt heute eine neue Blüte, die im ausgefallenen, eklektischen Schmuck des Bauwerks sehr gut zum Ausdruck kommt.

L'Ace occupe un ancien hôtel, le Breslin, dans un bâtiment de 1908 ; comme ses autres voisins, les modifications dans le quartier avaient marqué la fin de son heure de gloire. Cependant, la zone connue sous le nom de NoMad (Nord de Madison Square) est en plein renouveau, qui se reflète dans la décoration éclectique de l'hôtel.

Het Ace bevindt zich in het voormalige Hotel Breslin, in een gebouw uit 1908. Door veranderingen in de wijk kwam er een eind aan de gloriejaren van dit hotel. Het gebied dat nu bekendstaat als NoMad (North of Madison Square), maakt een wederopbloei door die te zien is in de eclectische versiering van het hotel.

EAT

Aspen Social Club 19

157 West 47th Street

Lewis & Dizon Collective
www.lewis-dizon.com

Colorado's sophisticated rustic chic is the predominant note in the interiors of this 2,900-sq ft restaurant and lounge. The decoration includes pieces by recognized artists, including a Jason Miller's spectacular spider light, made from antlers, hanging from the ceiling.

Der ausgeklügelte rustikale Chic von Colorado ist die vorherrschende Note in der Innenausstattung dieses Restaurants und der 270 m² umfassenden *Lounge*. Zur Ausschmückung gehören Werke anerkannter Künstler. So wurde der unglaubliche Kristalllüster aus Geweihen von Jason Miller gestaltet.

La sophistication chic et rustique de Colorado est la note qui prédomine dans les intérieurs de ce restaurant-lounge de 270 m². La décoration comprend des œuvres d'artistes connus, comme le spectaculaire lustre fait avec des ramures, œuvre de Jason Miller.

Het rustieke, chique raffinement van Colorado overheerst in de interieurs van dit restaurant annex loungeruimte van 270 m². De versiering bevat stukken van gerenommeerde kunstenaars, zoals de spectaculaire kroonluchter van een gewei aan het plafond ontworpen door Jason Miller.

EAT

Adour Alain Ducasse [20]

2 East 55th Street

Rockwell Group
www.rockwellgroup.com

© Eric Laignel

Adour is a restaurant and wine bar created by the famous chef Alain Ducasse in the mythical St Regis Hotel. The architects have managed to create an atmosphere as rich and complex as the wine served here, with the superimposition of spaces and textures, the richness of the materials and the integration of technology.

Restaurant und Weinbar „Adour" wurden vom berühmten *Chef* Alain Ducasse im legendären Hotel St Regis eingerichtet. Die Architekten haben eine Atmosphäre geschaffen, die ebenso reich und komplex ist wie ein Wein: Hier überlagern sich verschiedenartige Räume und Oberflächen, es gibt eine große Vielfalt an edlen Materialien und dabei wurde auf keine technische Neuerung verzichtet.

Adour est un restaurant et un bar à vins créé par le célèbre chef Alain Ducasse, dans le mythique hôtel St. Regis. Les architectes ont réussi à créer une ambiance aussi riche et complexe que le vin servi ici, grâce à la superposition d'espaces et de textures, la richesse des matériaux et l'intégration de la technologie.

Adour is een restaurant en *wine bar* ontworpen voor de beroemde chef-kok Alain Ducasse van hotel St. Regis. Met de boven op elkaar geplaatste ruimten, de rijke materialen en benutte technologie zijn de architecten erin geslaagd een sfeer te scheppen die even rijk en complex is als wijn.

RELAX

The Core Club (21)

66 East 55th Street

SPaN
www.span-ny.com

© Michael Moran

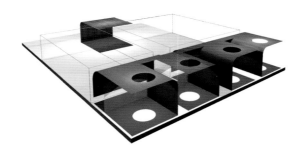

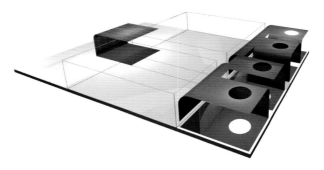

Spa treatment rooms

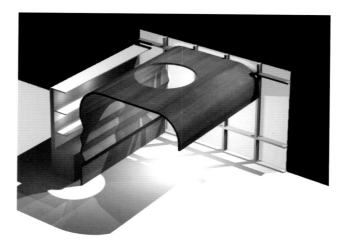

Stair diagram

This elite spa is distributed over five floors. The communal spaces, such as the theatre, the restaurant and the meeting room, are close to the entrance. The more personalized spaces, used for treatments, are located on the upper levels.

Dieses exklusive *Spa* erstreckt sich über fünf Geschosse. Die Gemeinschaftsräume – Theater, Restaurant und Veranstaltungsraum – befinden sich nahe dem Eingang. Dagegen bleiben die oberen Stockwerke den für jeden Gast spezifischen Anwendungen und Behandlungen vorbehalten.

Ce spa prestigieux est installé sur cinq étages. Les espaces communs, comme le théâtre, le restaurant et la salle de réunion se situent près de l'entrée. Les niveaux supérieurs, en revanche, ont été réservés aux espaces personnalisés consacrés aux traitements.

Deze chique spa is verdeeld over vijf verdiepingen. De gemeenschappelijke ruimten, zoals het theater, het restaurant en de ontmoetingsruimte, bevinden zich dicht bij de ingang. Op de bovenste verdiepingen zijn de persoonlijker ruimten te vinden waar behandelingen worden gegeven.

EAT

Pio Pio Restaurant (22)

610 10th Avenue

Sebastian Mariscal
www.sebastianmariscal.com

© Paúl Rivera

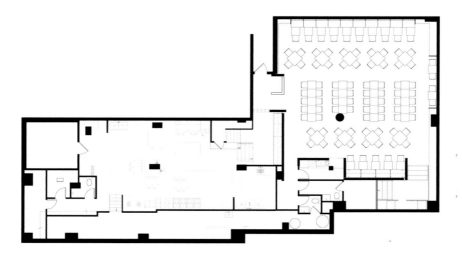

Lower plan

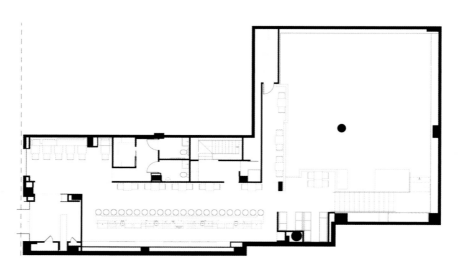

Upper plan

This Peruvian restaurant located in Hell's Kitchen is made up of four boxes built like installations. Three of them are clad in wood and the other in interwoven branches from an ocotillo bush.

Dieses peruanische Restaurant liegt im Viertel Hell's Kitchen und besticht durch die Einstellung der vier originellen Kästen, von denen drei mit Holz verkleidet sind und der vierte mit geflochtenen Ästen des Ocotillo-Strauchs.

Ce restaurant péruvien situé dans la zone de Hell's Kitchen se compose de quatre structures construites comme des installations, trois d'entre elles sont revêtues de bois et la dernière de branches entrecroisées de l'arbuste ocotillo.

Dit Peruaanse restaurant in de wijk Hell's Kitchen bestaat uit vier blokken die als installaties zijn opgebouwd. Drie ervan zijn met hout bekleed, het andere is bekleed met ineengevlochten takken van de ocotillo-struik.

LEARN

The NYC Information Center 23

810 Seventh Avenue

WXY Achitecture
www.wxystudio.com

© Albert Vecerka/Esto, Paul Warchol

This center replaced the desk with an information area using a combination of new technology and architecture. The physical and digital elements were designed to present the NYC-Go website and provide users with a novel experience.

In diesem Zentrum wird der Auskunftsschalter durch einen Informationsraum ersetzt, der Architektur mit neuen Technologien kombiniert. Sowohl die baulichen als auch die digitalen Elemente sind daraufhin ausgelegt, den Nutzern die Inhalte der Webseite NYC-Go auf ungewohnte Weise nahe zu bringen.

Cette installation remplace le bureau d'accueil par un espace d'information au moyen d'une combinaison de nouvelles technologies et d'architecture. Les éléments physiques et numériques ont été conçus afin d'offrir les contenus du site Internet NYC-Go et de fournir une expérience différente aux utilisateurs.

In dit centrum is de balie met een combinatie van nieuwe technologieën en architectuur vervangen door een informatieruimte. De fysieke en digitale elementen tonen de inhoud van de website NYC-Go en bieden de gebruikers een nieuwe ervaring.

LIVE

Urban Townhouse (24)

324 East 51th Street (between First Street and Second Avenue)

Peter Gluck and Partners Architects
www.gluckpartners.com

© Thomas Gluck, Bethia Liu, Aaron Sherbany

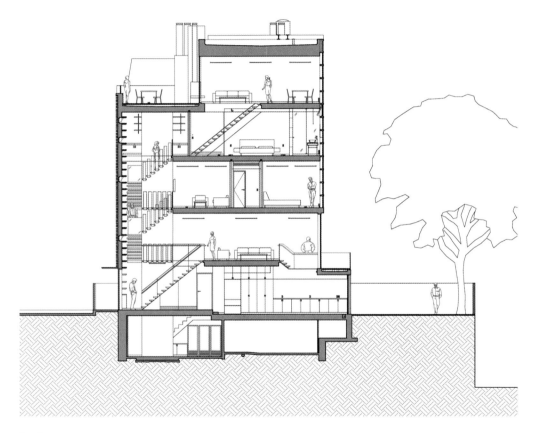

Section

This project was the extension of a house on an extremely narrow lot. The staircase, the elevator and a continuous wall with bookshelves, which runs the height of the four floors, provide privacy from outside.

Das besondere an der Erweiterung dieses Hauses ist das äußerst schmale Grundstück. Die Treppe, der Aufzug und eine durchgehende Wand mit Bücherregalen, die sich durch alle vier Geschosse zieht, schützen gegen neugierige Blicke von außen.

Ce projet est l'agrandissement d'une maison à trois étages sur un terrain extrêmement étroit. L'escalier, l'ascenseur et un mur continu avec une bibliothèque le long des quatre étages préservent l'intimité par rapport à l'extérieur.

Dit project betrof de uitbreiding van een huis op een uitermate smal terrein. Vanbuiten gezien zorgen de trap, de lift en een doorlopende boekenwand langs de vier verdiepingen voor privacy.

STAY

Renaissance Hotel Times Square 25

2 Times Square, 714 Seventh Avenue

Jordan Mozer and Associates
www.mozer.com

© Jeff Zaruba Photography

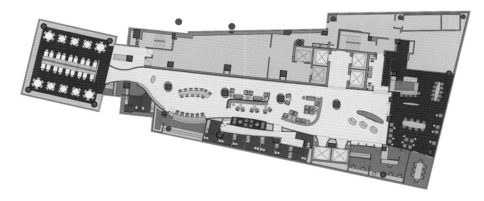

First floor plan

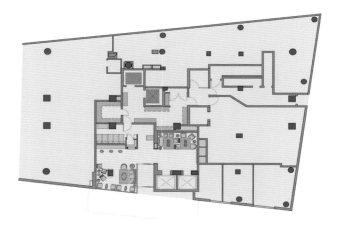

Second floor plan

Sensual shapes and made-to-measure furniture define the remodeling of this hotel, which needed to adapt to match the quality offered by other hotels in the area. The entrance on the first floor, the lobby on the second, two lounges, a bar and a cafeteria were all renovated.

Sinnliche Formen und speziell entworfene Möbel bestimmen die Renovierung dieses Hotels, dessen Ausstattung an die heute herrschenden Standards angepasst wurde. Erneuert wurden die Eingangshalle, die *Lobby* im zweiten Stock sowie zwei Lounges, eine Bar und eine Cafeteria.

Des formes sensuelles et des meubles sur mesure caractérisent la rénovation de cet hôtel, qui devait s'adapter afin d'atteindre la qualité de l'offre hôtelière du quartier. L'entrée du rez-de-chaussée, le lobby au premier étage, ainsi que deux lounges, un bar et une cafétéria ont été transformés.

Dit hotel werd gerenoveerd omdat het zich moest meten met het nieuwe hotelaanbod in dit gebied. Het resultaat wordt gekarakteriseerd door sensuele vormen en op maat gemaakte meubels. Op de eerste verdieping werd de entree gerenoveerd, op de tweede de lobby, twee lounges, een bar en een lunchroom.

WORK

Michael Neumann (26) Architecture Office

127 West 24th Street

Michael Neumann Architecture
www.mnarch.com

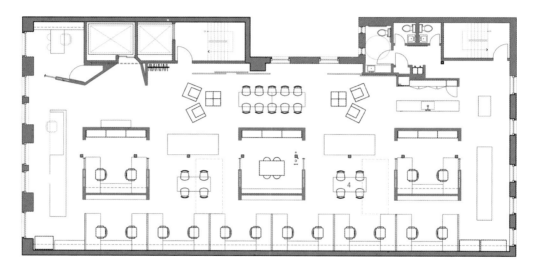

Floor plan

Michael Neumann Architects set up their new offices in an old industrial building which they reformed themselves. The three cubicles in the center house offices and a conference room, and are partially open to the communal spaces.

Das Büro Michael Neumann bezog seine neuen Arbeitsräume in einem ehemaligen, von den Architekten selbst renovierten Gewerbegebäude. Die drei eingestellten Kästen nehmen Büros und einen Besprechungsraum auf und sind gegenüber den Gemeinschaftsräumen geöffnet.

Le bureau d'architectes de Michel Neumann a installé ses nouveaux bureaux dans un ancien édifice industriel réaménagé par ses soins. Les trois cubes au centre abritent des bureaux et une salle de conférence et ils restent partiellement ouverts sur les espaces communs.

De nieuwe kantoren van het bureau van Michael Neumann werden in een voormalig industrieel gebouw gevestigd dat het bureau zelf had gerenoveerd. In de drie middelste ruimten bevinden zich werkkamers en een vergaderzaal, die gedeeltelijk open zijn naar de gemeenschappelijke ruimten.

LIVE

Madison Square (27)

Madison Square Park

Desai/Chia Architecture
www.desaichia.com

© Paul Warchol

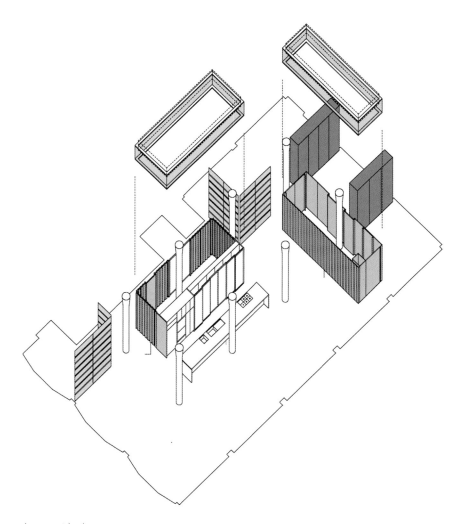

Axonometric view

This large, bright apartment is the result of the renovation of an old, dark loft. The property is arranged around two perpendicular structures which house a bathroom, a kitchen and spaces for storage whilst creating privacy in the bedrooms.

Aus einem alten dunklen Loft wurde nach einer durchgreifenden Erneuerung ein helles weitläufiges Appartement. Die Wohnung ist in zwei, im rechten Winkel zu einander liegende Bereiche getrennt. Es gibt ein Bad, eine Küche und Lagerräume. Die Schlafzimmer sind Privatsphäre.

Ce grand appartement lumineux est le résultat de la rénovation d'un ancien loft sombre. La demeure s'articule autour de deux structures perpendiculaires, qui abritent une salle de bain, une cuisine et des espaces de rangement, tout en préservant l'intimité des chambres.

De renovatie van een oude, donkere loft leidde tot dit lichte, ruime appartement. De woning is ingedeeld rond twee verticale structuren. Hierin bevinden zich een badkamer, een keuken en bergruimten. Bovendien waarborgen de structuren de privacy van de slaapkamers.

SHOP

TKTS Booth (28)

Times Square

Perkins Eastman; Choi Ropiha; William Fellows/PKSB
www.perkinseastman.com
www.choiropiha.com
www.pksb.com

© Wade Zimmerman, John Saeyong Ra, Jack Mussett, Ari Burling

Original Booth © Van Alen Institute

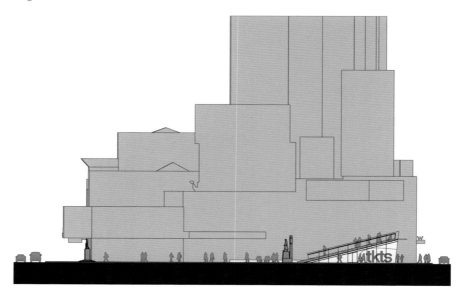

Elevation

The traditional stand selling tickets for shows on Broadway in Times Square has been replaced by a platform which shines at night and looks like the seats at a theatre – from here the spectacle of the city can be enjoyed.

Der traditionelle Verkaufsstand am Times Square für Eintrittskarten der Veranstaltungen der Broadwaybühnen ist durch eine Plattform ersetzt worden, die nachts erleuchtet wird und an das Parkett eines Theaters erinnert, von dem aus man das Schauspiel der Stadt bewundern kann.

Le stand traditionnel de vente d'entrées pour les spectacles de Broadway sur Times Square a été remplacé par une plate-forme qui brille pendant la nuit et qui ressemble au parterre d'un théâtre à partir duquel il est possible d'assister au spectacle de la ville.

Het traditionele ticketverkooppunt voor de Broadwayvoorstellingen op Times Square is vervangen door een platform dat 's avonds oplicht en doet denken aan de stalles van een theater vanwaaruit men het spektakel van de stad kan bijwonen.

STROLL

High Line 29

Gansevoort Street to 34th Street, between 10th & 11th Avenues

James Corner Field Operations, Diller Scofidio + Renfro, Piet Oudolf
www.fieldoperations.net
www.dillerscofidio.com
www.oudolf.com

© Joel Sternfeld
Drawings design by James Corner Field Operations and Diller Scofidio + Renfro. Courtesy of the City of New York

The old high line

Sections

This park is a mile and a half long and has been created on abandoned elevated train tracks. The project, the first stretch of which is located in the Meatpacking District and is already finished, combines areas in which to walk or rest with green spaces comprising a great variety of plants.

Dieser eineinhalb Meilen lange Park wurde auf ehemaligen Bahnanlagen angelegt. Der erste Teil des Projekts im Meatpacking District ist bereits fertig gestellt und umfasst Spazierwege, Ruhezonen und Grünanlangen mit einer großen Vielfalt an Pflanzen.

Ce parc long de 2,4 km a été créé sur les voies désaffectées d'un train. Le projet, dont le premier tronçon sur le Meatpacking District est déjà achevé, combine espaces de promenade et de repos avec des espaces verts composés d'une grande variété de plantes.

Dit park van anderhalve mijl lengte ligt op een verhoogd treintraject dat niet meer in gebruik was. Het eerste gedeelte in het Meatpacking District is al voltooid. Het park heeft zowel gedeelten waar kan worden gewandeld en gerecreëerd, als groene ruimten met een grote variëteit aan planten.

UPTOWN

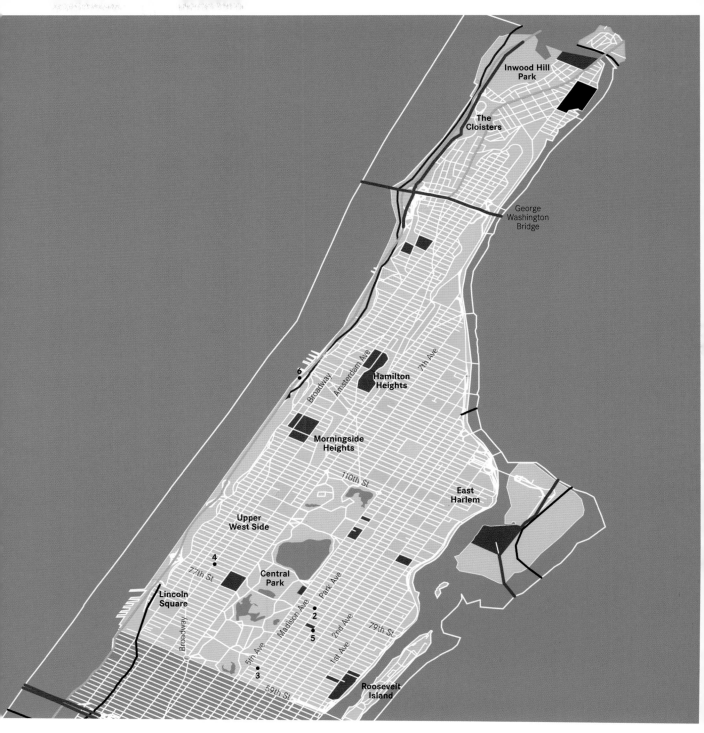

Inwood Hill
Park

The
Cloisters

George
Washington
Bridge

6

Broadway

Amsterdam Ave.

7th Ave.

Hamilton
Heights

Morningside
Heights

East
Harlem

110th St

Upper
West Side

Central
Park

4

77th St

Lincoln
Square

Broadway

5th Ave.

Madison Ave.

Park Ave.

2

5

2nd Ave.

1st Ave.

79th St

3

59th St

Roosevelt
Island

STAY

Plaza Hotel ①

768 Fifth Avenue

Remodelling: Costas Kondylis and Partners
www.kondylis.com

© Plaza Hotel

This mythical New York hotel was remodeled and now has opened again after two years. The work included installing new technology and restoring legendary spaces such as the Oak Bar, the Palm Court and the Plaza Grand Ballroom.

Das berühmte New Yorker Hotel hat nach zweijähriger Umbauphase seine Pforten wieder geöffnet. Während der Bauarbeiten wurde nicht nur die Haustechnik völlig erneuert, sondern auch legendäre Einrichtungen wie die Oak Bar, der Palm Court oder der Plaza Grand Ballroom restauriert.

Ce mythique hôtel new-yorkais a rouvert ses portes après une rénovation qui a duré deux ans. Les travaux ont compris l'installation de nouvelles technologies et la restauration d'espaces légendaires comme l'Oak Bar, le Palm Court et le Plaza Grand Ballroom.

Dit mythische New Yorkse hotel heeft na een twee jaar durende renovatie zijn deuren weer geopend. De werkzaamheden omvatten onder meer de installatie van nieuwe technologieën, plus de restauratie van legendarische ruimten zoals de Oak Bar, het Palm Court en de Plaza Grand Ballroom.

SHOP

Lilly Pulitzer (2)

1020 Madison Avenue

Michael Neumann Architecture
www.mnarch.com

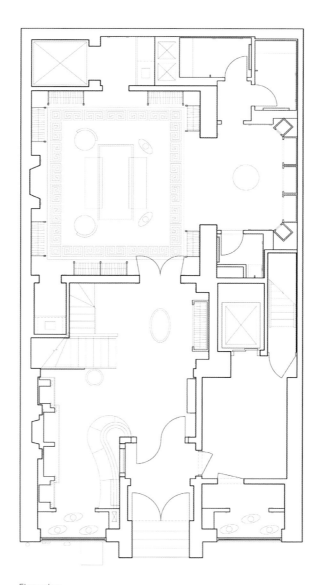

Floor plan

The design of this shop, which is located in a house built in 1912, aimed to highlight the period features. Plaster molding and original wooden panels were exposed, and a careful restoration was carried out to create a chic style which reflects the brand.

Bei der Einrichtung des Ladengeschäfts in einem Gebäude von 1912 wollte man die Details der Originalausstattung so weit möglich nutzen. Deshalb wurden die Stuckleisten an der Decke und die Holzverkleidung wieder freigelegt und mit sorgfältiger Restaurierung versucht, einen zur Firma passenden Stil zu entwickeln.

Le design de ce magasin, situé dans une maison de 1912, a voulu tirer le meilleur parti possible des détails d'époque. Des moulures en plâtre et des panneaux en bois d'origine sont désormais apparents, un travail soigneux de restauration a été effectué pour obtenir un style chic, en adéquation avec l'image de la marque.

Bij het ontwerp van deze winkel in een huis uit 1912 wilde men zoveel mogelijk profiteren van de typische details uit die tijd. Er werden pleisterwerk en originele houten panelen blootgelegd, die met grote zorg werden gerestaureerd om tot de chique stijl te komen die past bij het merk.

SHOP

Mauboussin Flagship Store ③

714 Madison Avenue

Rockwell Group
www.rockwellgroup.com

© Barbel Miebach

MAUBOUSSIN

This shop is located in a renovated house. The objects are arranged in original display cabinets which capture the magic of the brand in a surreal environment full of unexpected designs.

Das Geschäft befindet sich in einem renovierten Altbau. Die Waren werden in originellen Ausstellvorrichtungen präsentiert, die den Zauber des Firmennamens in einem surrealistischen Ambiente mit unerwarteten Designelementen aufleben lassen.

Le magasin est situé dans une maison rénovée. Les objets sont disposés dans des présentoirs originaux, qui capturent la magie de la marque dans un environnement surréaliste plein de designs inattendus.

De winkel bevindt zich in een gerenoveerd huis. De objecten worden tentoongesteld in originele ruimten die de magie van het merk in een surrealistische omgeving vol onverwachte ontwerpen weten te vangen.

SHOP

Malin+Goetz Apothecary ④

455 Amsterdam Avenue

Craig Konyk
www.konyk.net

© Eric Laignel

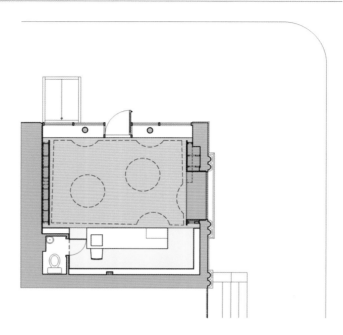

Floor plan

Elevations

In order to adapt the Upper West Side's elegant style to this old mansion on Long Island, wooden cladding with a Belle Époque air has been used. The perforations in the panels house shelves, in imitation of the building's exterior windows. The result is a warm, contemporary space.

Um sich dem eleganten Stil der Upper West Side anzupassen, wurden die Innenräume dieses alten Herrenhauses auf Long Island im Stil der Belle Époque mit Holz vertäfelt. In den Nischen der Vertäfelung sind Regale untergebracht. Entstanden ist ein einladender Raum in zeitgenössischer Ästhetik.

Pour s'adapter au style élégant de l'Upper West Side, des revêtements en bois de style Belle Époque ont été utilisés dans cette ancienne demeure de Long Island. Les perforations dans les panneaux ont permis d'y placer des étagères et elles imitent une des fenêtres extérieures du bâtiment. Le résultat obtenu est un lieu chaleureux et contemporain.

Om te passen bij de elegante stijl van Upper West Side zijn in dit voormalige herenhuis op Long Island bekledingen van hout in belle-époquestijl gebruikt. De openingen in de panelen herbergen rekken en lijken op een van de ramen van het gebouw. Het resultaat is een warme, hedendaagse ruimte.

WORK

The Vilcek Foundation Headquarters ⑤

167 East 73rd Street

Tow Studios Architecture
www.towarchitecture.com

© Bjorg Magnea

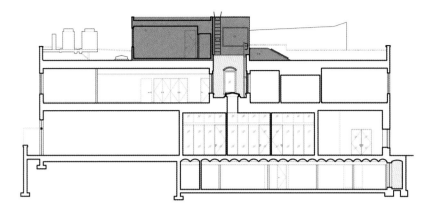

East longitudinal section

Elevations

The minimalist style of the interiors produce the wide, open spaces required by the Foundation, which awards prizes to foreigners who stand out in arts and science. The façade has been restored with the classic elements of the typical buildings on the Upper East Side.

Der Minimalismus der Innenausstattung ergab sich aus der Notwendigkeit weite, offene Räume zu schaffen, so wie sie sich die Stiftung wünschte, die Ausländer auszeichnet, die sich in Kunst oder Wissenschaft hervorgetan haben. An der Fassade wurden die für die Gebäude der Upper East Side charakteristischen Elemente restauriert.

Le style minimaliste des intérieurs répond au besoin de grands espaces ouverts de la Fondation qui récompense les étrangers se distinguant dans les arts ou les sciences. La façade a été restaurée avec les éléments classiques des bâtiments typiques de l'Upper East End.

Het minimalistische interieur beantwoordt aan de behoefte van deze stichting aan ruime, open ruimten. De stichting reikt prijzen uit aan buitenlanders die zich onderscheiden in de kunst of de wetenschappen. De gevel is gerestaureerd met klassieke elementen uit voor de Upper East Side typerende gebouwen.

STROLL

West Harlem Piers Park ⑥

125th Street and 135th Street, Broadway and the Hudson River

W Architecture and Landscape Architecture
www.w-architecture.com

© Johannes Feder, Barbara Wilks, Alison Cartright, Tatiana Choulika

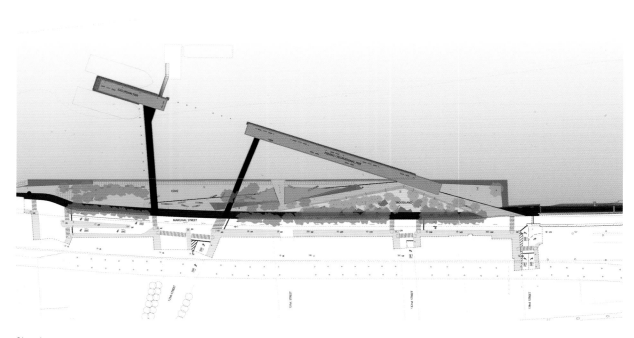

Site plan

This park is located on the site of an old car park, and connects the community with the Hudson River. It includes a stretch of bicycle path (which completes the route that runs around the whole island next to the coast) new piers, diagonal paths and surfaces with geometrical shapes which visually open the space.

Der Park ist anstelle eines ehemaligen Parkplatzes entstanden und verbindet ein Wohnviertel mit dem Hudson Fluss. Er umfasst einen Radweg entlang dem umlaufenden Uferweg, neue Kaimauern, Querwege und geometrisch gestaltete Flächen, die den Raum optisch erweitern.

Ce parc occupe le site d'un ancien parking et relie la communauté au fleuve Hudson. Il comprend une piste cyclable (qui complète le chemin qui fait le tour de l'île près de la côte), de nouveaux quais, des chemins en diagonale et des surfaces avec des formes géométriques qui ouvrent visuellement l'espace.

Dit park is aangelegd op een voormalig parkeerterrein en verbindt de wijk met de rivier de Hudson. Er loopt een fietspad doorheen, een aanvulling op de kustweg rondom het hele eiland. Er zijn nieuwe kades, diagonaal lopende paden en geometrische gevormde delen die de ruimte visueel vergroten.

BOROUGHS

New Jersey

Bronx

4

1

Manhattan

3

5

Queens

2

Brooklyn

6

Staten Island

LIVE

Bronx Box ①

3272 Tierney Place

Resolution: 4 Architecture
re4a.com

First floor plan

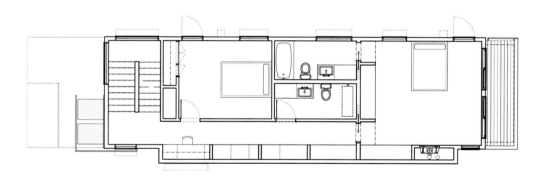

Second floor plan

This prefabricated house has a parking space, a terrace on the roof, a green area and a jetty facing the Throgs Neck Bridge. The property is made from panels of cement and wood, which reduces maintenance to a minimum and integrates it with its surroundings.

Dieses Wohnhaus aus Fertigteilen verfügt über einen PKW-Stellplatz, eine Dachterrasse, einen Grünbereich und eine Anlegestelle gegenüber der Throgs Neck Brücke. Der Bau passt sich gut in die Umgebung ein; er wurde aus Betonplatten und Holzpanelen errichtet, die nur geringe Wartungsarbeiten erfordern.

Cette demeure préfabriquée dispose d'un parking, d'une terrasse sur le toit, d'une zone verte et d'un embarcadère situé en face du Throgs Neck Bridge. La maison se compose de panneaux en ciment et en bois afin de réduire au minimum la maintenance et de la relier esthétiquement à son environnement.

Deze prefabwoning heeft een parkeerplaats, een dakterras, een groen gebied en een aanlegsteiger die tegenover de Throgs Neck Bridge ligt. Het huis bestaat uit panelen van cement en hout. Die behoeven nauwelijks onderhoud en verbinden het huis esthetisch gezien met de omgeving.

EAT

High School Cafeteria ②

Bushwick HS 480, 400 Irving Avenue

a+i architecture
www.aplusi.com

© a+i architecture

Existing space

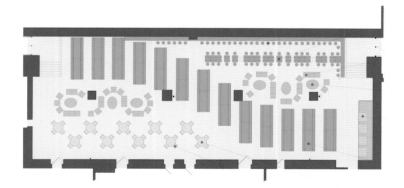

Furniture plan

In collaboration with the Bill and Melissa Gates Foundation, the television channel MTV and the organization New Visions for Public Schools, the cafeteria in this high school has become an attractive, modern space where students can come to eat or to carry out academic activities.

In einem Gemeinschaftsprojekt der Stiftung von Bill und Melissa Gates, dem Fernsehsender MTV und der Organisation New Visions for Public Schools wurde die Cafeteria dieser Oberschule zu einem modernen, attraktiven Aufenthaltsraum umgestaltet, den die Schüler nicht nur während der Mahlzeiten, sondern auch zur Erledigung der Hausaufgaben nutzen können.

En collaboration avec la fondation de Bill et Melissa Gates, la chaîne de télévision MTV et l'organisation New Visions for Public Schools, la cafétéria de ce lycée est devenue un espace moderne et plaisant, destiné à recevoir les élèves à l'heure des repas ou à leur permettre d'effectuer des activités scolaires.

In samenwerking met de stichting van Bill en Melissa Gates, MTV Television en de organisatie New Visions for Public Schools is de kantine van deze onderwijsinstelling veranderd in een moderne, aantrekkelijke ruimte waar studenten kunnen eten en waar onderwijsactiviteiten kunnen plaatsvinden.

SEE

MoMA/PS1 ③

22-25 Jackson Avenue at the intersection of 46th Avenue

MOS
www.mos-office.net

© Wade Zimmerman

Each year the PS1 Contemporary Art Center and the Museum of Modern Art organize a competition to present an innovative project. In 2009 the winner was MOS with an installation of chimneys which provide cool air by induction, helping to refresh those attending the summer music sessions in the courtyard.

Jedes Jahr schreibt das dem MoMA angeschlossene PS1 Contemporary Art Center einen Wettbewerb für innovative Projekte aus. Im Jahre 2009 war das Büro MOS der Gewinner: Der Vorschlag bestand in der Errichtung einer Art Schornsteine, die den Innenhof der Einrichtung während der Musikveranstaltungen im Sommer kühlen.

Le bâtiment le plus proche de l'emplacement où se trouvaient les tours jumelles est un gratte-ciel de 52 étages, qui marque l'entrée du complexe du World Trade Center. La surface de la tour a été conçue comme une « peau » qui respire et s'adapte aux besoins de ventilation.

Het PS1 Contemporary Art Center organiseert elk jaar een wedstrijd om een innovatief ontwerp te kunnen presenteren. In 2009 was studio MOS de winnaar met een installatie van schoorstenen die met inductie het plein koel hielden tijdens zomerse muziekvoorstellingen.

READ

NYPL Francis Martin Library ④

2150 University Avenue

1100 Architect
www.1100architect.com

© Timothy Furze

Section

This children's reading room has been designed to stimulate the imagination and encourage learning through colors and shapes. Bold, eye-catching graphic elements have been used, which stand out against the curved, bright white surfaces.

Die farbenfrohe, formenreiche Gestaltung des Kinderlesesaals soll zur Lese- und Lernförderung und der Anregung der Fantasie beitragen. Daher wurden einprägsame grafische Akzente gesetzt, die auf den gewellten, glänzend weißen Oberflächen besonders ins Auge fallen.

Cette salle de lecture pour enfants a été conçue afin de stimuler l'imagination et d'encourager l'apprentissage par la couleur et la forme. Dans ce but, des éléments graphiques étonnants et voyants, qui se remarquent sur les surfaces ondulées de couleur blanche brillante, ont été utilisés.

Deze kinderleeszaal is ontworpen om de fantasie en het leerproces via kleur en vorm te stimuleren. Er zijn daarom uitgesproken, opvallende grafische elementen gebruikt waarvan de golvende, glanzend witte vlakken de aandacht trekken.

LISTEN

Kemado Records ⑤

87 Guernsey Street

SPG Architects
www.spgarchitects.com

© SPG Architects

Architects remodeled an old industrial building to create recording studios and offices for a music label. The distribution of the spaces was changed, up-to-the-minute technology installations were incorporated and new cladding was fitted, but the style of the old building was preserved.

Die Architekten haben ein altes Gewerbegebäude umgebaut, um ein Tonstudio und die Geschäftsräume eines Musikverlages unterzubringen. Die Raumaufteilung wurde völlig neu gestaltet und die neuesten technischen Errungenschaften bei den Versorgungsleitungen und den Wandverkleidungen genutzt. Trotz allem blieb die Ästhetik des Altbaus weitgehend erhalten.

Les architectes ont réaménagé un ancien bâtiment industriel pour le transformer en studios d'enregistrement et en bureaux pour un label musical. La distribution des espaces a été modifiée, des installations dotées de la dernière technologie ont été mises en place mais l'esthétique de l'ancienne structure a été conservée.

De architecten hebben een voormalig industrieel gebouw veranderd in de opnamestudio's en kantoren van een muzieklabel. De ruimten zijn anders ingedeeld, de nieuwste technologische installaties werden geplaatst en nieuwe bekledingen werden aangebracht, maar de esthetiek van het gebouw is gehandhaafd.

SEE

Brooklyn Botanic Garden Visitor Center 6

1000 Washington Avenue

Weiss/Manfredi
www.weissmanfredi.com

Drawings: © Weiss/Manfredi

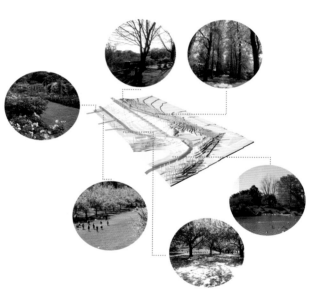

Details

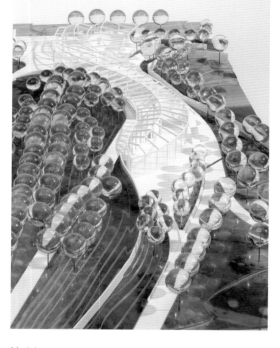

Model

This building, at the entrance to the Botanical Gardens, is the Information Center. Its winding shape follows the line of the paths in the garden. The curved walls of porous glass which make up the façade filter the light and afford spectacular views of the gardens. The temperature inside the building is regulated by a geothermal system of hot and cold air.

Am Eingang des Botanischen Gartens steht dieses Informationszentrum, dessen geschwungene Form an die Wegführung im Garten erinnert. Die gebogenen, durchlässigen Glaswände der Fassade filtern das Tageslicht und erlauben den Blick hinaus in den Garten. Die Innentemperatur wird über eine Geothermik-Anlage geregelt.

Ce bâtiment se trouve à l'entrée du Jardin Botanique et du Centre d'information. Sa forme tortueuse suit le tracé des chemins dans le jardin. Les murs courbes en verre poreux sur la façade filtrent la lumière et offrent des vues spectaculaires sur le jardin. La température interne du bâtiment est maintenue grâce à un système géothermique d'échange d'air froid et chaud.

Bij dit gebouw beginnen de botanische tuin en het informatiecentrum. Zijn kronkelige vorm imiteert de slingerende tuinpaden. De ronde muren van geperforeerd glas filteren het licht en bieden een goed uitzicht op de tuin. De temperatuur in het gebouw wordt op peil gehouden met een geothermaal systeem.

CLASSICS

1   Brooklyn Bridge/John Augustus Roebling

The Trump Building (former 40 Wall Street)/H. Craig Severance

3   Flatiron Building/Daniel Burnham

4   United Nations Headquarters / Le Corbusier, Oscar Niemeyer, Sir Howard Robertson, et al. with Harrison & Abramovitz

Empire State Building/Gregory Johnson

6   Chrysler Building/William van Alen

7   RCA Building at Rockefeller Center/Raymond Hood

8   Seagram Building/Ludwig Mies van der Rohe

World Financial Center / César Pelli & Associates

0   Museum of Modern Art (MoMa)/Yoshio Taniguchi

11   Lipstick Building/John Burgee Architects

3   Woolworth Building / Cass Gilbert

14   Saint Patrick's Cathedral / James Renwick, Jr.

GGENHEIM   MUSEUM

15   Solomon R. Guggenheim Museum/Frank Lloyd Wright

16   Trump Tower/Der Scutt

17   Carnegie Hall Tower/César Pelli & Associates

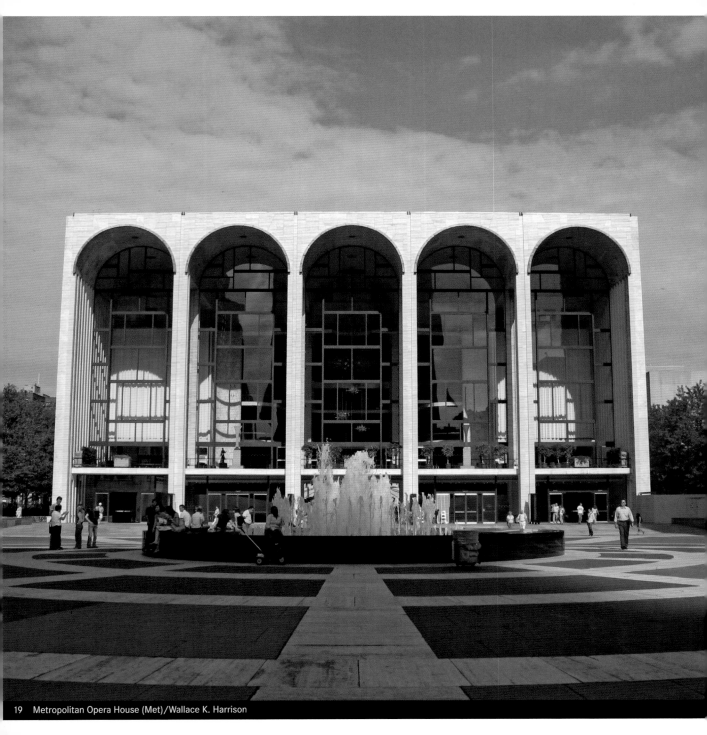

19 Metropolitan Opera House (Met)/Wallace K. Harrison

Time Warner Center/David Childs and Mustafa Kemal Abadan/Skidmore, Owings & Merrill

21   McGraw-Hill Building/Harrison, Abramovitz & Harris

23 New York Life Building/Cass Gilbert

24 MetLife Building/Emery Roth & Sons

25 TWA Terminal/Eero Saarinen

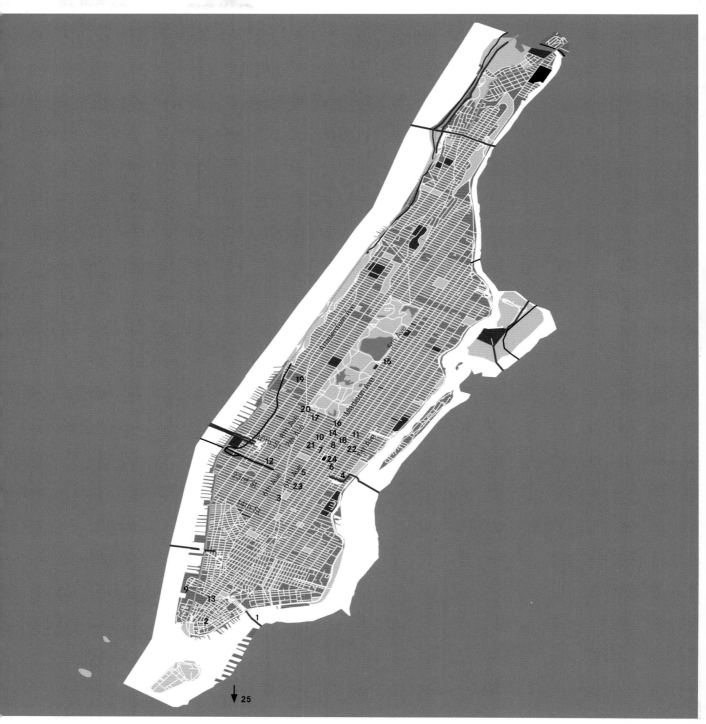

19

20

17
16

14 11
10 18
21 8 22
J
24
5 6
23 4
3

15

Amsterdam Ave

5th Ave

Madison Ave

3rd Ave

8th Ave
7th Ave

10th Ave
9th Ave

6th Ave

23rd St

14th St

12

9
13
2 1

↓ 25

Photo Credits